FALLEN
OFFICERS
Canadian Police in the Line of Fire

FALLEN
OFFICERS
Canadian Police in the Line of Fire

Peter Boer

QUAGMIRE
PRESS

© 2008 by Quagmire Press Ltd.
First printed in 2008 10 9 8 7 6 5 4 3 2 1
Printed in Canada

The Publisher: Quagmire Press Ltd.
Website: www.quagmirepress.com

Library and Archives Canada Cataloguing in Publication

Boer, Peter, 1977–
    Fallen officers / Peter Boer.
ISBN 978-0-9783409-4-0

    1. Police murders—Canada. 2. Police—Canada—Death. 3. Police—Canada—Biography. 4. Royal Canadian Mounted Police—Biography. I. Title.

HV7911.A1B63 2008   363.2092'271   C2008-905708-2

Project Director: Peter Boer
Project Editor: Kathy van Denderen
Production: Alexander Luthor
Cover Image: Courtesy of JupiterImages
Photos: Courtesy of Lyle Aspinall/*St. Albert Gazette* (pp. 191, 197)

PC: P1

Contents

"Greater love has no one than this, that he lay down his life for his friends."

Acknowledgements

None of this work would have been possible without the encouragement and extraordinary patience of my mom. To my editor Kathy van Denderen for again daring to tackle one of my books—it'll get to you on time one day. To my colleagues Ryan Tumilty and Lyle Aspinall for sharing their memories—you are both talented in your crafts. To the *St. Albert Gazette* for allowing the use of its photos. To my partner Kathy, for her love, support and understanding throughout this process, and to Christopher, for giving me a reason to smile on days when I needed it most.

Introduction

The men and women described in this book are heroes. They are not heroes because they died in the line of duty. They are heroes because of what they did when they lived.

As a journalist, it never ceases to amaze me how the death of a police officer, regardless of what province they serve in, what force they are attached to or the circumstances surrounding their death, resurrects a nationwide pride for the men and women who "serve and protect." Communities cry together, create memorials in their honour, provide comfort and support for the families left behind and ultimately grieve the loss as poignantly as any loved one.

There is, it seems, no greater act that can trigger public outrage than to kill a police officer in the line of duty, and rightfully so. We depend on our police every day of every year to respond to our complaints and our concerns, defend our communities from the underworld tangles of crime and provide safety and security to our children. We see them out of uniform coaching our hockey and baseball teams, dedicating their off-duty time to directing traffic for charity walks or runs or raising money for causes of their own by shaving their heads or coming up with their own ideas. They volunteer overseas to train police in developing nations and provide assistance in times of crisis. When Mother Nature unloads, they are the ones who stay behind to make sure everyone else has left.

And, in rare instances, they put their own physical bodies between the evil in the world and the good that requires protection. Too often it seems, especially since the turn of the 20th century, police officers come out on the losing end of that confrontation. South of the border, police officers are merely becoming targets for criminals. And the same situation is happening here in Canada as well. Often it is the local media in the U.S. that report the stories of an officer's death, but the national media—such as CNN—are quick to jump on a story from our country anytime one of our best dies in the line of duty. Violence, it seems, is not a cultural organ of being Canadian, so when it happens, the rest of the world finds it newsworthy.

Canada has had a national police presence for over 100 years, since the March West of the North-west Mounted Police (NWMP), to protect the settlers. The vision synonymous with policing, of course, is that of the descendants of the Northwest Mounted Police—the Royal Canadian Mounted Police (RCMP) with their formal red serge, Stetsons and riding boots.

But as far-reaching as the RCMP may be, they do not police the entire country. Provinces such as Ontario and Québec have their own separate provincial and municipal police forces, while larger cities have created their own police departments. The colours each force wears, formally or informally, may differ, but their cause is shared. That's why, whenever a police officer dies in Canada, thousands of other peace officers—some even from other countries—descend on the community for the funeral and memorial service. Justice is more than a principle; it's a bond shared by everyone who wears a uniform.

Punishments for those who kill police officers in Canada have been the subject of debate—with every killing comes another suggestion that capital punishment be re-instated for those who kill police officers. Over 30 years ago, Parliament started weaning the country away from executions when there were two different punishments for first-degree murder—the murder of any peace officer was considered a capital offence, while the murder of any other citizen was not. Now that capital punishment has been abolished in Canada, that distinction still holds true. Any person alleged to have killed a police officer is automatically charged with first-degree murder, regardless of whether the homicide was planned or not. First-degree murder carries the stiffest penalty possible in Canada—life in prison, with no possibility of parole for 25 years.

Who are these people who feel so threatened by the police that they feel justified in shooting them? The research bears out some common trends. Every offender and alleged offender described in this book either has a criminal background or is somehow involved in criminal activity. Some are described as loners with a palpable hatred for the police, who feel persecuted by their very presence, even though it's the person's own background that brings them into the focus of the police. Some are mentally ill. Some love guns. Some are criminals who just don't want to go back to jail, and in one instance the individual was just confused about what was going on. Every person depicted in this book, convicted or not, felt somehow persecuted by the police. In those cases that have gone to court or that have been reviewed after the fact, that feeling of being targeted by police somehow does not stand up to outside scrutiny.

The most tragic and heart-wrenching case, with the highest loss of human life, is the Mayerthorpe shootings of March 2005. James Roszko, a convicted pedophile with a history of harassing, stalking and filing unproven complaints against members of the rural RCMP detachment, fled from his property when two bailiffs showed up to repossess a truck. Despite Roszko's reputation as a violent man and a known police hater who hid guns all over his property, two officers were left to guard the marijuana grow-op and chop shop found inside the infamous Quonset hut on his land. Two more officers joined them later that morning. Somehow Roszko returned to the property, got into the hut and killed all four officers inside. Ultimately Roszko took his own life. The case continues, however, as two men face charges of first-degree murder for somehow aiding Roszko in his slaughter.

Curtis Dagenais was also known as a loner and a man who hated the police, a belief many residents of Spiritwood, Saskatchewan, say came from his father. Allegedly, a dispute over his parents' matrimonial property led to a confrontation with police and a high-speed chase. In the end, Constables Robin Cameron and Marc Bourdages were left dead, and the suspect in the shootings fled the scene on foot. After an 11-day manhunt, Dagenais turned himself into police. At the time this book was written, he was scheduled to go to trial in September 2008.

Martin Ostopovich shared similar qualities with Dagenais and Roszko—he hated the police, loved guns and lived an isolated life—but with one major exception. Ostopovich was mentally ill. It might have been that illness that led to a standoff with the RCMP in the Edmonton suburb of Spruce Grove. Corporal James Galloway was a veteran RCMP dog handler, charged with responding to any scene that called for an RCMP Emergency Response Team (ERT). When the ERT converged on Ostopovich's home and negotiations failed, Ostopovich tried to leave. Galloway and another officer rammed the man's truck, but Galloway was shot dead when he tried to exit the vehicle. The rest of the ERT converged on the vehicles, killing Ostopovich as well. No one will ever know what was going through Ostopovich's mind when he decided to open fire on a police officer.

Robert Sand believed that he was at war. The career criminal, in conjunction with his brother, and girlfriend Laurie Bell, engaged in an extended crime spree that started in Alberta and moved on to Manitoba. Believing the three were making their way towards a new life somewhere out East, Robert even wrote that anyone who tried to stop them would be sorry. That individual turned out to be Constable Dennis Strongquill, a longtime RCMP officer, who, along with partner Brian Auger, pulled over Sand's stolen vehicle outside Russell, Manitoba. When Strongquill approached the vehicle, Sand opened fire. The two officers fled back towards their detachment, but not before Sand followed them, boxed in their truck and fired several bullets into Strongquill, killing him instantly. The manhunt that followed left Sand's brother dead, and Robert Sand and Laurie Bell were charged with first-degree murder.

Constable Christopher Worden was killed in Hay River, Northwest Territories, in 2007, and after an extended manhunt, suspect Emrah Bulatci was arrested in Edmonton and charged with Worden's death. Many of the circumstances surrounding the case are still unknown, but they may come to light when Bulatci goes to trial.

Most intriguing is the case of Laval Constable Daniel Tessier, shot to death by Basil Parasiris, a businessman and self-confessed drug dealer. In a high-risk drug raid gone horribly wrong, Parasiris shot Tessier to death before surrendering. He never denied killing Tessier, but maintained throughout his trial that he did not know he was shooting at a police officer; he claimed he was just defending himself and his family from a potential home invasion. Based on the evidence tendered at trial, the jury believed him, and Parasiris was acquitted based on self-defence. The verdict doesn't mean that Parasiris didn't kill Tessier—he did. His acquittal is simply a legal technicality.

The circumstances surrounding each case require intensive research to tell the story in a complete, accurate and respectful fashion. Common themes can also be found in the personality of each offender, alleged or otherwise, as well as the reaction or mistakes made by the police, and the dedication to duty and public service each officer portrayed in this book demonstrated every day.

Ultimately, the one theme that links all six chapters is guns—a firearm killed all of the officers. Most police officers are not shot to death while on duty—they are more often the victim of a car accident, either when pulling over a vehicle or manning a roadblock a driver doesn't want to stop for. Yet the number of gun crimes against police, from anecdotal evidence, seems to be increasing. All of the shootings described in this book took place within the last seven years, and the officers portrayed are not the only officers who have been shot to death while on duty.

On December 14, 2005, Laval Constable Valérie Gignac and her partner received a noise complaint at the apartment of François Pepin, a man already convicted of uttering death threats. He was under a court order not to possess any firearms, but a clause in the order allowed him to have a rifle for hunting. Pepin fired a shot through the door. The round ripped through Gignac's bulletproof vest, killing her.

Constable John Atkinson was a 14-year veteran of the Windsor police, dressed in plain clothes on the afternoon of Friday, May 5, 2006, when he approached two men in a local convenience store parking lot. The 37-year-old officer, suspicious that a drug transaction was occurring, was gunned down in the parking lot. Atkinson was holding his badge in his hand when he was hit. He managed to return fire but did not hit anyone. Atkinson's murder was the first time a police officer with the Windsor Police Department had been killed in the 120-year history of the force. Eighteen-year-old Nikkolas Brennan was charged, and a jury eventually found him guilty of first-degree murder in a trial that featured a dispute over whether or not Brennan knew Atkinson was a police officer. He was sentenced to life in prison with no possibility of parole for 25 years. Coty Defausses, the other man in the parking lot, was originally charged with first-degree murder as well, but the charge was dropped, and he instead pleaded guilty to possession of crack cocaine for the purpose of trafficking and received a 20-month sentence.

Constable Douglass Scott, 20, of Brockville, Ontario, was on duty in Kimmirut, Nunavut, on November 5, 2007, when he responded alone to a report of a drunk driver in the hamlet on Baffin Island. Two local residents found his body—

he had been shot at approximately 11:30 PM local time and died of his injuries. Investigators later revealed that Scott was shot before he could even get out of his car. Witnesses said Scott took no visible action when faced with an armed man because the man was holding a young child. Scott had graduated from Depot in Regina the previous spring and had served at the detachment in Kimmirut for only six months. After a three-and-a-half-hour standoff, a suspect surrendered to police the day after the shooting. Pingoatuk (Ping) Kolola, 37, was charged the following day with first-degree murder. On August 18, 2008, after a preliminary hearing, a judge ordered Kolola to stand trial. No date has yet been set.

Our police are supposed to be our very best citizens, and most often they are. Their chosen career means deliberately placing themselves in harm's way every single patrol, not knowing what awaits them when they don their uniforms. The most dangerous situation any police officer faces is a simple roadside stop of a vehicle for speeding or for having expired tags. Officers approaching vehicles have no idea who or what is waiting for them inside the vehicle.

Dennis Strongquill died as a result of a routine roadside stop. Before Robert Sand's trial began, his lawyer tried to argue that the charge of killing a police officer shouldn't automatically be first-degree murder simply because a police officer was the victim. While Sand's lawyer may have just been trying to give

INTRODUCTION

17

his client the best possible defence, it is difficult to agree with such an assessment, and the judge thankfully threw out the argument. Police officers deserve to be recognized for the commitment they make to public safety and to our communities. Anyone who thinks their life is worth more than an officer's should spend the rest of their life behind bars.

There is some fault within each story in this book that does not belong to the killers—the actions individual officers took contributed to the situation; the policies in place offered little or no support for the police; there was inadequate equipment for the scenario at hand or just poor judgement on the part of the officers involved. Hindsight is always perfect, but all the would haves, should haves and could haves in the world can't correct what happened in each case. At the moment of their deaths, the officers described within this book were doing the best job they could with the training and resources available to them. No police force can plan for the actions of every single individual or the outcome of every single scenario. In most of these cases, the sacrifice these officers made, whether directly or indirectly, saved the lives of others.

My heart goes out to the immediate and extended families of all the officers whose names appear in this book and the loved ones of all who have died in the line of duty. No one can imagine the pain and loss they must have felt at the time and still feel to this day. It might be reassuring for those left behind to know the enormous sacrifice these fallen officers made for their communities, but at the end of a long day, when you're standing alone in an empty room, it is difficult to imagine what kind of comfort that knowledge can bring. That refrain may be true, but no one wants to have to live through it.

It is my hope that I have done these officers justice in this work. They, and every other police officer who has died in the line of duty, will forever have my thanks.

Chapter One

Constable Dennis Strongquill

Killed: *December 20, 2001, Waywayseecappo,
Manitoba*
Accused: *Robert Marlo Sand, Laurie Ann Bell*
Charge: *First-degree murder*
Status: *Robert Marlo Sand guilty—First-degree
murder; sentenced to life in prison; Laurie Ann
Bell guilty—Manslaughter;
sentenced to seven years, released March 2008*

~

June 12, 2003

I t was now or never.

He stared out from the prisoner's box of the Brandon, Manitoba courtroom, taking in the scene around him. The atmosphere was relatively quiet and relaxed. The court had adjourned for lunch some time ago, and only now everyone was starting to trickle back in for the continuation of the court's proceedings. His lawyers were back, the Crown prosecutors were back, and even his fiancée was back, seated in her prisoner's box right next to his.

The only people who hadn't returned from lunch yet were arguably the most important. The jury was still excused, sequestered in a room somewhere eating lunch, while the judge overseeing the case had yet to return.

The courtroom was humming with mindless activity as family, spectators and reporters chatted back and forth, waiting for the last day of the trial to begin. It had been a long one, almost 10 weeks in duration. And in that 10 weeks, the accused had been on his best possible behaviour, even though it was killing him inside.

Ten weeks of testimony, evidence and audiotape. Ten weeks of hearing about how evil he was, how awful his fiancée was. Ten weeks of repeated references to the death of his brother. All of that testimony, combined with spending the last 18 months imprisoned, had taken its toll. It would only take one action to bring all his rage rushing to the surface.

He'd known for the longest time that he was going to do something. Now, even as he sat in the prisoner's box, his legs shackled but his hands unrestrained, he knew he'd never get another chance because today was the day the jury would be sent away to debate his case and deliberate his fate. That he was going to jail was a foregone conclusion—it was just a matter of how long. Whether or not his fiancée would also end up incarcerated was something he had tried hard to prevent.

The final wound in the entire ordeal had come from one of the Crown prosecutors. As the court broke for lunch, the lawyer glanced towards him and actually smirked; he actually dared taunt the man whose actions were mostly responsible for bringing everyone here for the last 10 weeks. It was more than he could bear, the last straw. Of course, he was prepared.

He knew that the guards at the Brandon Correctional Institute where he was being held during the trial had been freaking out for the last few weeks, trying to find the razor blade that had gone missing somewhere in the prison population. Stealing it hadn't been difficult, and concealing it was even easier. He knew they'd searched his room and found nothing— well, they'd found his diary and all of the letters he and his fiancée had managed to secretly exchange during this ordeal. That didn't help his case any. But they hadn't found the razor.

There was only one problem with his plan—someone was in the way. The person wasn't someone he wanted to hurt, but this was war. It was him against the system, and sometimes in war there are innocent casualties. He wasn't sure exactly what he was going to accomplish, but he just knew he had to do something.

There were only a few minutes left; lunch would be over, and the courtroom would be full again. Now was the time to strike. He slowly stood up from his bench and used his hands to lift himself up onto the gate of the prisoner's box. No one seemed to be paying him any attention, which was good. He leapt from the gate to the floor and, despite the shackles on his ankles, managed to keep his footing. Unfortunately, he couldn't move quickly or deftly. He stumbled on his first few steps then piled onto the back of the man who was in the way, the man he really didn't want to hurt. The defence lawyer crumbled beneath his attacker's weight, and both collapsed to the ground in a thrash of arms and legs. The impact jarred the razor blade loose, and he felt his grip on it slip, then suddenly realized he wasn't even holding it anymore. That was unfortunate, but he was prepared.

He had a back-up weapon, one the guards and authorities couldn't do anything about. After all, grooming was a personal choice. And if he chose to grow his left thumbnail several inches long and file it down to a point, so be it. There was nothing they could do.

He had the man in his grips now and could hear the sheriffs guarding the courtroom rushing towards him, could hear his fiancée screaming as she was dragged away from the courtroom. He hoped she'd understand. He wasn't just doing this for himself. He was doing it for her too.

He felt hands grab at him, but he shrugged them off, brought his left thumbnail up to the lawyer's neck and started applying pressure.

"Let me go or I'll cut his throat," yelled Robert Sand, the man charged with first-degree murder in the killing of Constable Dennis Strongquill.

December 2001

He knew who she was the second he saw her.

Robert Sand was doing some last-minute running around in downtown Edmonton, just happy to be away from the half-way house that had been running his life for the last several months, telling him where he could or could not go and what time he had to return. He was getting away, though. He was going to spend Christmas in Westlock, a small town less than an hour's drive northwest of Edmonton. It would be the first Christmas in a long time that the entire family would actually be together, and Robert was kind of looking forward to it. He'd applied for and received a pass from the Stan Daniels Healing Centre, and he was planning to make the most of it.

And then he saw Laurie Bell, standing at a bus stop downtown, stoned out of her mind.

He knew Laurie. And by saying he *knew* Laurie Bell was to say that he knew Laurie Bell in the biblical sense. She'd been maybe 15 at that party many years ago when they'd met, partied and had sex. She'd been a demon back then, but any lingering passion she may have had seemed obscured in a haze of drugs.

He didn't have much time. He was supposed to meet a family friend, but looking at Laurie, he felt he had to do something for her. So Robert went up to her and spoke her name. The eyes that stared back at him were foggy and uncomprehending. The temperature was well below freezing, and she was hardly dressed for the weather. To Robert's eyes she looked awful. In his mind, she was his salvation.

In that instant, Robert knew he was going to help this girl. He was going to get her off drugs. He was going to help her get back on track. He was going to do everything he could to bring her around.

He barely had to say anything, and Laurie quickly fell into step beside him. Robert's brother Danny lived close by; he'd get some hot food into her, and she could get some rest.

~

Constable Dennis Strongquill was the happiest he had ever been in his life.

He was 52 years old but felt as invigorated as someone half that age. He was a father for the sixth time—and a grandfather four times over no less—but he felt like it was the first time all over again. He was divorced twice, but he was in love like he had never known before. Life was finally smiling on Dennis Strongquill.

He loved where he was—Manitoba, where few people, let alone Mounties, wanted to serve. But the province was home to Strongquill, and he was happy to serve in Waywayseecappo, a small Native community 30 kilometres east of Russell. Strongquill was Aboriginal and felt a kinship with the reserve municipality. Sure he was three years away from 55, but why contemplate ever retiring?

Life had not been particularly kind to Dennis; some of his experiences were more heart wrenching than fulfilling.

His parents had abandoned him at a powwow in Saskatchewan when he was only a few weeks old. The Genaille family had been kind enough to take him in, raising him in Red Deer Lake, north of Barrows, Manitoba. When he reached the age of 30, he tracked down his birth mother. She told him she had no choice but to abandon him because she was afraid her boyfriend at the time would kill her. Dennis' relationship with his birth mother was just starting to blossom when she died of complications from diabetes.

It wasn't the only heartache Strongquill had known in his life. After all, he'd already had two heart attacks, both of them minor. He'd been married for 18 years to Collette Aubine, with whom he'd had three beautiful children—Teresa, Joey and Ricky. Their split had been amicable. Shortly afterwards he'd married Donna, but that marriage too came to an end.

As well as coping with these breakups, Strongquill was plagued by the same disease that claimed the lives of many of his First Nations brothers and sisters, the effects of which Dennis saw on almost a daily basis at work—alcoholism. It had gotten really bad after he and Donna split in 1997, the depression so deep and dark that it seemed the only exit was through the open mouth of a liquor bottle. But he'd battled back. After he and Donna divorced, it took Dennis only a year to go dry. And he hadn't gone back.

Dennis had known exactly what he wanted to do with his life from a young age. The red serge of the RCMP had been running through Strongquill's veins since he was eight years old, when he first saw the Mounties walking in a parade in their characteristic red tunics, navy pants and Stetsons. When he was old enough, he was hired as the band constable in Barrows to help offset the lack of an RCMP presence in the community. After years of patrolling the community, he was offered a position with the national police force. In his shortened career, Strongquill had already served in different communities, such as Churchill, where the polar bears often came out to play, and was now in Waywayseecappo. He'd helped out during the Winter Olympics in Calgary, Alberta, in 1988, enjoying the rush of policing a world-class event. Now he was working in the area around Russell, mostly in Waywayseecappo, part of a special unit that helped patrol the reserve area. Crime really wasn't that big a problem, but connecting with the local Native community was. And Dennis, with his visible heritage, was a perfect fit.

Of course, his mind these days was not focused solely on policing. At the age of 52, when most men started diligently planning their retirements and looking for recreational property, Dennis had become a father. He was head-over-heels in love with his girlfriend, Mandy Delorande, and the news that she was pregnant had been like music to his ears. Only six weeks earlier, Mandy had given birth to Korrina, a beautiful baby girl. Dennis fell madly in love with her the second the nurses passed her to him.

It had been easy to love Mandy because she understood where Dennis had come from, having battled drug and alcohol addictions in her own past. Now they were parents. He was looking forward to spending Christmas with Mandy and Korrina, along with his other children. It was going to make for a full house, but Dennis couldn't think of anything that could possibly make him happier.

It was December 20, and Christmas was only five days away. Mandy and Korrina were finally home. Dennis had spent the bulk of the last few days working and making the rounds, spreading as much Christmas cheer to co-workers and friends as he could. It seemed as though Mandy and Korrina had barely arrived home when he had to bolt out the door at 6:00 PM to work the evening shift. He was scheduled to ride with Constable Brian Auger, a man Strongquill knew well. Plus it was freezing outside, and the snow this year had fallen hard. Even as he drove to meet up with Auger, Dennis knew it was going to be a quiet night.

At 7:30 PM Dennis snuck away from his shift and headed home, sharing a pot roast dinner with Mandy. After his meal, he returned to work, but there was so little to do that he made his way home again at 10:00 PM. He and Mandy spent some time playing cards, simply reveling in one another's company. After an intense game of crib, Dennis crept into Korrina's room and for a few moments watched the tiny infant sleep. She was beautiful.

So was Mandy. He kissed her goodbye and told her he'd see her when he was off shift at 2:00 AM. Then he headed out to meet Auger.

It was the last time Mandy saw him alive.

～

At midnight on a cold winter night, there are few treats as valuable as a cup of hot coffee.

All was quiet in Waywayseecappo that December night in 2001, and no matter how often Dennis glanced at the clock on the dashboard of the RCMP Ford Explorer, the minutes didn't seem to move any faster. So with no incidents to respond to, he and Auger accepted the invitation from fellow member Constable Jennifer Pashe to meet her at the Subway in Russell for a cup of coffee. It seemed like the perfect way to peel off a few minutes from their shift.

Strongquill and Auger weren't in Russell yet, so they radioed back to Pashe that they would meet her at the sandwich restaurant. It was quiet in the SUV, with Auger driving and Strongquill riding shotgun. They'd been talking almost all night, and it seemed they'd finally run out of things to discuss. Dennis blinked his eyes to fight off the fatigue and looked at the dashboard clock again. It had barely moved.

The tires hummed on cold asphalt as the pair drove west along Highway 45, both flicking their eyes around the surrounding countryside for anything they needed to respond to.

CONSTABLE DENNIS STRONGQUILL

29

Suddenly, a truck approached the intersection at Highway 45, peeled through the plainly visible stop sign and turned east on 45. Both officers flinched as the truck flew past, its high beams nearly blinding them.

They'd have to be a bit late for coffee. Auger slowed the vehicle and pulled a U-turn, activating his overhead emergency lights and accelerating as the pair took off after the truck. As soon as the two officers were within the truck's sight lines, it started to slow down, then pulled to the side of the highway and stopped. Auger and Strongquill pulled up behind the truck, noting the Alberta licence plates screwed to the rear.

Auger stayed in the driver's seat while Strongquill unclipped his seatbelt and threw open the passenger's side door of the SUV, cringing against the frosty temperatures. The SUV's headlights illuminated the truck, while the overhead lights cast shadows of blue, white and red in random circles.

Just as Strongquill's feet hit the asphalt, a figure emerged from the passenger's door of the truck. Strongquill frowned— most people knew to stay in their vehicle during a traffic stop until the police approached. The practice was as much a safety measure for the occupants as the police. A traffic stop is one of the biggest risks in the policing world, simply because the officer walks into a situation blind and vulnerable. Whoever was in the truck had run a stop sign and left their high beams on. It seemed innocent enough, but police officers worldwide die because they pull over the wrong vehicle at the wrong time.

The man who got out of the truck now approached the police SUV, just out of the range of the truck's headlights. Strongquill was about to warn him to stay where he was when the roar of a shotgun shattered the quiet of the winter's night.

Dennis lunged back into the SUV as another boom split the night, splashing a spider web design across the windshield of the SUV.

"Back up! Back up!" Dennis yelled at Auger as two more loads of buckshot rebounded off the SUV. Auger was already in motion, slamming the SUV into reverse and stomping the gas. He yanked the wheel hard, bringing the SUV about, and stomped on the gas again, taking off for Russell. Auger reached down and flipped a button, activating an emergency beacon that broadcasted from the SUV throughout the area.

Strongquill looked over his shoulder, and his mouth practically dropped open. The truck they had pulled over had also turned around and was actually chasing them.

The two officers weren't running away so much as looking for reinforcements and buying time. They had no idea what or who they were dealing with, and the person who had opened fire on their vehicle already had the upper hand. Both Auger and Strongquill were equipped with their sidearms, but they hadn't grabbed the dash-mounted shotgun from the detachment when they started their shift. They were already outgunned. The best plan, they concluded, was to head into the Russell detachment for shelter, reinforcements and bigger guns.

Auger's speedometer topped 130 kilometres per hour as the SUV roared towards town, but the truck was still pursuing them, still gaining on them. There were more booms and cracks from behind, as Dennis, crouched low in his seat, grabbed his handheld radio. A dispatcher in Winnipeg was hailing him, wondering why their emergency beacon had sounded.

"There's a vehicle following us," Strongquill gasped into the radio. Suddenly the rear window of the SUV disintegrated as another shot found its mark.

"We're hit!" Strongquill yelled into the radio.

Auger plowed through the night towards Russell as Dennis reached down for his sidearm. Dennis felt the gun come free, then his heart sank as he heard the ammunition in his automatic fall to the floor. Dennis, unlike the majority of RCMP officers in the force, was a left-handed shot. They didn't make holsters for left-handed shots, meaning he had to put a regular holster on his left side. The position of the gun in the holster was awkward and unfortunate—as Strongquill yanked at his gun, the ammunition mechanism caught on the holster, releasing the clip, which scattered his bullets all over the floor of the SUV. He had no time to grope around in the dark for it. Instead he clung to his radio.

"Shot at, we're being shot at, guys. We're being shot at. You hear that…shootin' us. They're still shootin' us," he said.

Auger and Strongquill tersely discussed their plan. They would drive as close as possible to the Russell detachment, then both bail out of the SUV and head for the doors, hoping there were other officers inside, or at least more powerful weapons. Auger drove into Russell at a faster speed than anyone in the town ever had. He headed up Main Street, watching the truck in the rearview mirror cut the distance, and listened to the smack of bullets and buckshot ricocheting off the Plexiglas barrier separating the front and back seats.

The detachment was just ahead, a shining beacon in a desperate hour. But Auger drove past the entrance, turning into a snowy ditch to try to turn around. He slammed on the brakes as a thick line of trees barred his forward progress.

The truck, which had been chasing them for what felt like an eternity, did not stop, but instead slammed into the SUV's passenger's side.

The impact was jarring and forceful. One minute Auger was right beside Strongquill and the next minute he was gone, thrown from the vehicle in the violent collision. Strongquill twisted and turned in his passenger's seat, thrashing desperately to get free or grab his sidearm. Another crack split the night, and just as quickly, Strongquill lurched as a bullet struck him, followed by another and another. The last one tore into his back.

Then Dennis Strongquill felt nothing.

Auger was now up and moving. He'd seen the muzzle flashes, but couldn't see Dennis anywhere. He reached down and unholstered his Smith & Wesson 9 mm automatic, snapping it out as he rushed around the SUV to the driver's side of the truck that had rammed them. He noted three people inside but concentrated his aim on the driver's side, hoping to take out the person behind the wheel. His finger started yanking on the trigger over and over again as he fired shot after shot. Sparks flew as the bullets smacked against the metal body of the truck. The vehicle started to pull away, and Auger kept firing, hoping to tag someone inside before they could get away. In total, Auger fired 12 rounds from his sidearm.

But it didn't appear to have any effect. Even after Auger's volley, the truck sped off towards the highway, seemingly unaffected by his actions.

The truck receded into the back of Auger's mind as he dove towards the passenger's side of the SUV. He yelled Dennis' name and shook him vigorously, but there was no response. His fingers desperately crawled under Strongquill's chin and then at his wrist, feeling for a pulse; there was none. He raised his radio to his lips.

"Down, member down."

Auger had just made the radio call when Constable Jennifer Pashe arrived, the member with whom they were supposed to have coffee. She'd heard the initial calls for help and had started making her way towards the detachment to lend assistance.

She didn't know as she pulled up to the scene that the shooters had sped past her in the opposite direction.

The scene in front of her was tragic. Dennis' head was face down on the console, his body unresponsive as Auger continued to try to shake him awake. An ambulance arrived, the crews quickly hauling Strongquill from the SUV and tearing off, lights and sirens blazing.

But it was too late. Dennis Strongquill was dead.

～

The call that officers were under fire and the updated situation report from the scene of the fatal confrontation was broadcast to police units all over Manitoba. Off-duty members, especially those in the area surrounding Russell, were called out to start manning roadblocks throughout the area.

By now, word that Strongquill was dead started to trickle through the force, generating a strong emotional response. The RCMP members in Manitoba were committed to tracking down whoever had killed one of their own.

Squad cars were dispatched to the main and secondary highways in the western part of the province in the hopes of containing the suspects before they got too far away. Constable Matthew Lavallee was posted at the intersection of Highways 83 and 482, watching for any suspicious activity. Suddenly two trucks flashed past him. Sensing he was on the right track, Lavallee took up the chase and radioed for help. He stayed behind the two trucks until they turned onto a gravel road that wound down a hill. Lavallee stopped his cruiser at the top of the hill. He was familiar with the area, and he knew the road dead-ended at the bottom of the hill. The suspects were trapped.

Constable Jennifer Pashe, still shaken from what she had seen in Russell, arrived to back up Lavallee, the two of them waiting on top of the hill for more assistance. They heard the roar of a powerful engine and watched as one truck, not two, shot past them back onto the highway. Lavallee took off in pursuit, but the Silverado was travelling too fast and had too much of a head start. Before they knew it, the vehicle was gone.

They radioed ahead that the truck was heading west towards the Saskatchewan border. The Mounties had already set up a roadblock in the tiny hamlet of Shellmouth on the Saskatchewan side of the border. With a little less than two hours having passed since Strongquill's killing, a truck roared towards them and again blew by. The officers at the roadblock took up the chase, but quickly slammed on the brakes as the sounds of two gunshots from the suspect vehicle stopped them in their tracks.

All the RCMP could do was watch helplessly as the Chevy Silverado disappeared into the night.

~

A tip came, of all places, from a motel.

Jerry Olm, co-owner of the Wolseley Motel in Wolseley, Saskatchewan, had just finished his early-morning shift of working the front desk and was on his way to his son's garage when he noticed several police cars in the area, many more than usual. When he arrived at his son's, he happened to mention what he had seen. His son informed him that a police officer in Manitoba had been killed and that the police were looking for the shooters, who were reportedly driving a grey truck, but that was later amended to be a red truck.

Olm quickly put his morning together in his mind. He had indeed seen a red truck. The occupants had come in that morning, asking for a room and an 11:00 AM wake-up call. One of the men had been covered in dried blood. The other said their vehicle had broken down near the Manitoba border and a friend had lent them a truck. They'd lost their ID and needed a room to rest for a few hours. The man pulled out a $100 bill, so Jerry wasn't about to say no. Their story sounded strange, but they had money for the room. The man who had done all the talking signed the register "Bill M. Wright," then walked out to the truck and started unloading bags.

Olm reached for his son's phone. Within seconds, Olm's tip was being broadcast to RCMP forces across the area. Lawrence Shier, a customs' officer driving through the area, radioed in that he would check it out. He took a spin past the Wolseley Motel and spotted the red truck. After Shier reported the sighting, the RCMP asked him to remain on scene and to watch the vehicle.

Manitoba's RCMP Emergency Response Team was immediately called to the scene to deal with the situation. While a couple of plain blue SUVs took up positions outside the motel to keep an eye on the room and the truck, the rest of the team deployed throughout the area. The motel and nearby restaurant were evacuated. Snipers set up their high-powered rifles at points all around the motel, including a gas station and a farmer's field, where a shooter was concealed behind a bale of hay.

Sixteen officers descended on the motel. The Trans-Canada Highway, which zipped right past the front of the building, was shut down in both directions, frustrating the efforts of holiday travellers trying to get to their destinations in time for Christmas. With everyone in place, the officers on scene could do nothing but wait. The motel room did not have a telephone, so there was no chance to call and negotiate with the occupants.

The few hours that passed seemed to stretch into an eternity, but everyone came to sharp attention at 2:24 PM when movement was spotted at the room's window—the flicker of a curtain pulled back then left to fall back into place.

Moments later, snipers watched as one young man emerged from the rear window of the motel room and, instead of heading for the ground, climbed up onto the roof. They also noticed the rifle in his hands. The man took up a position on the rooftop, staring down the scope of his rifle and surveying the scene around him.

Sniper Kelly Painter, stationed on top of a nearby gas station, tried to radio in what he saw, even though everyone else saw it too. The man on the roof was pointing his rifle at the position where another sniper was posted. Unfortunately, someone's radio was malfunctioning, and Painter could not get his message through. Faced with these aggressive actions, and with only split seconds to act, Painter fired two shots at the man's head, followed by three more. A sixth shot from another sniper nearby barked as well. All of them missed their mark.

The shots, however, were instantly misconstrued by the officers on the ground.

Sniper Al Lukasewich had taken up position behind some bales of hay. "Half a dozen shots fired from the subject!" he radioed out, watching as the man on the roof skipped from the motel roof to the roof of a nearby building.

Lukasewich believed the man had already fired on police and was ready to act.

"We're gonna take him out," Lukasewich said.

He received the go-ahead heartbeats later from the officer in charge of the scene. The shot was easy as the man was in plain view. Lukasewich took aim at the subject's head and fired one shot. There was an explosion of blood and tissue, then the body instantly crumpled on the rooftop.

~

Officers on the ground waited apprehensively. Already a man and woman had come running around the corner of the motel, but when faced with the police presence and calls to halt, they retreated to the rear of the motel. The tension grew thicker as the bark of a shotgun erupted from behind the motel. Moments later, officers heard the crack of another rifle along with a call over their radios, despite a pair of terrified screams from the rear of the building.

"Badger's down on the roof. Badger's down on the roof. He's not moving. He's not moving."

The officers on the ground were at the ready, firearms drawn, waiting either for the order to move in or for the subjects to come out shooting. Instead, a woman came around the corner of the motel, her hands held high in the air. Seconds later, a young man followed. The officers swarmed the pair, forcing them to the ground, handcuffing them, patting them down, then taking them to separate squad cars.

Their identities were quickly established. The man was Robert Sand, 23, of Westlock, Alberta. The woman was Laurie Bell, 20, of Athabasca, Alberta. The man on the roof was Robert's younger brother Danny, 21.

The officers on scene decided to take the two suspects to the nearby detachment at Indian Head for questioning. As the cruiser carrying Robert pulled away, the quiet, blond-haired man offered only one thought.

"You guys ruined my birthday."

～

The officers on the roof of the building adjoining the motel approached the body of Danny Sand cautiously. He was obviously dead, but you couldn't be too careful.

Danny's T-shirt had crept up after he'd fallen. As several officers gathered to move the body, they caught sight of a tattoo on the dead man's stomach—"Fearless. Painless. Senseless."

～

Robert and Danny Sand had spent most of their life growing up in Westlock, Alberta, a small town approximately an hour northwest of Edmonton. Their life had not been easy, but compared to others, it hadn't been that bad either. They moved around a lot as youngsters as their father Dennis tried to find steady work and distance himself from the convictions for breaking and entering he had racked up. He was a Grade 10 dropout who worked everywhere he could, first on a farm and then as a welder. Eventually, Dennis found a steady job with the Town of Westlock, and the family settled down in a trailer home just outside town limits. Dennis' wife Elaine ran a karaoke business and tried to keep a neat home for Robert, Danny and their younger brother Dusty.

Yet for all their efforts, trouble was never far behind Robert and Danny. As teenagers, the older brother preferred stealing cars while Danny seemed to enjoy killing porcupines with pointed sticks. Neither had any interest in school, and both were suspended many times for fighting.

"They were trouble makers. They weren't well liked," one Westlock resident told the press.

In time, both Danny and Robert were doing drugs. They started smoking pot and eventually moved on to crack. As they grew older, their problems only deepened. Danny was sent to jail as a youth for breaking another kid's jaw when he overheard the victim calling Dusty a pussy. Dennis and Elaine tried putting Danny on Ritalin for a month but didn't like the zombie-like side effects. Robert was already stealing cars, often lighting them on fire afterwards, partly for the thrill and partly to destroy the evidence.

Robert's most serious encounter with the law came in April 1998. Robert, his then-girlfriend Sonja Boutin and a 15-year-old male were on their way to a house party. Once at the party, they decided they wanted beer and didn't have any money to get it. The youth and Robert devised an ingenious plan—they ordered pizza from a restaurant, waited for the driver to deliver it, then jumped him and stole his car.

The crime didn't end there, however. Over the next few days, Robert and the youth headed south, and when the car broke down, they set it on fire and stole a truck. When that truck stopped working, they torched it and stole another. After one more burning and one more stolen truck, they found themselves in Sylvan Lake, short on money and no way to get home.

To supplement their funds, Robert decided to rob a grocery store, fleeing with cash and cigarettes. A few days later, the trio found themselves in Fawcett, Alberta, again out of money. This time they hit a tavern, making off with $70 and six liquor bottles.

But the police were already onto them. The teenagers stopped to party at a gravel pit near Fawcett, and the police were waiting for them when they came out. The chase was on almost immediately. A squad of police cars trailed Robert and the group, while a chopper kept an eye on them from above. An officer ahead of the chase deployed a spike belt that punctured three of the truck's tires. Another police officer shot out the last one, but the truck continued rolling on its rims. The 15-year-old grabbed a gun from inside the truck, crawled into the back and opened fire on the police, who fired back. The youth responded by throwing the vehicle's spare tire and an empty beer bottle at the police chasing them.

Robert turned into a farmer's field but lost control of the stolen truck and smashed into a fence. A cruiser following right behind them didn't stop, colliding with the rear of the truck. The youths made a run for it, but in the end all were captured. Eventually, the 15-year-old snitched, and Robert was sentenced to seven years in prison. Sonja promptly dumped him.

Danny for his part was already following in his brother's footsteps, using drugs, decorating his body in tattoos and making threatening phone calls to an ex-girlfriend. In 1999, Danny and a friend confronted some people in a car who they felt had cut them off. Danny decided to up the ante by wielding a tire iron. When the police arrived, Danny punched one of the officers. He was given a brief jail sentence at Drumheller Institute and was released in the spring of 2000.

But Danny's freedom lasted only a few months. On June 5, 2000, an Edmonton police officer received a call about a suspicious vehicle on the city's north side. Danny was the driver of the vehicle, and when the officer got out of his cruiser to approach the truck, Danny decided to step on the gas. The officer leapt out of the way as the truck caromed off the police car. The police officer pulled his gun and fired a single shot at the fleeing truck. Danny was eventually caught and convicted of dangerous driving and possession of stolen property. He received a sentence of two years and two days, which he also served in Drumheller.

The boys' experiences in Drumheller were markedly different. Danny was released in 2001, before Robert, but only because Danny's sentence was shorter and he'd served two-thirds of it. At every opportunity, Danny had been denied parole.

"They expressed the fear that [he would] someday seriously injure or kill someone," stated one report on his file.

Robert, meanwhile, was trying to win the prison authorities over. He was on his best behaviour and seemed to be trying to improve himself, earning his high school diploma and construction safety certificate, as well as taking petroleum service training. He also completed anger management and cognitive skills classes. By the end of his sentence, Robert had been transferred to minimum security.

"His progress has been exceptional," his caseworker stated.

Eventually, Robert was granted parole, earning a bed in Edmonton's Stan Daniels Healing Centre halfway house. It was tough living under so many rules, but Robert was trying his best at the time to go straight. He worked odd jobs, followed the rules at the house as diligently as he could and tried not to cause any problems.

Danny seemed to be doing well too. He'd gotten off the hard drugs, but still smoked pot. He'd found work at a stockyard, fixing fences and herding cattle. He even lived with a roommate and diligently reported to his parole officer. As Christmas 2001 approached, the brothers were looking forward to spending their first Christmas in a long time with their entire family back in Westlock.

And then, one day in early December 2001, Robert ran into Laurie Bell.

Laurie Bell was just a teenager when she and Robert Sand first met at a house party in 1998. They'd partied and then had sex, even though Robert's girlfriend at the time was also at the party. Then Sand didn't see Bell for three years.

Bell's upbringing in Athabasca had also been less than perfect. Her parents were divorced, and she lived with her mother, who worked as nurse. Laurie had been a sweet girl, but slowly started getting into trouble as she approached her teen years. Her parents sent her to a home for troubled children, but when she returned, she was angry with them for sending her away. She dropped out of school in Grade 9 and hooked up with a guy who introduced her to crystal meth. She partied most of the time, staying with her father at the Union Hotel in Athabasca. Eventually, she found her way into Edmonton, couch-surfing and living with prostitutes. Her mother's only request was that she call once a week and let her know she was still alive.

By 2001, Laurie was a shadow of her former self. She was strung out on drugs, hooked to the rave scene and begging for money. On the December day that Robert saw her, she looked as if she'd been using speed all night long. Robert wanted to get her cleaned up, and she desperately needed help. And so their relationship began anew, with the most noble and simple of intentions.

Brandon, Manitoba

April 2003

Danny Sand was dead. Robert Sand and Laurie Bell were charged with first-degree murder in the death of Dennis Strongquill. It was time to go to trial.

The trial site was selected out of convenience. The town of Russell was too involved with the case, which meant that finding impartial jurors was unlikely. Winnipeg, the province's capital city, was too far away, so the trial was moved to Brandon, Manitoba.

Both Laurie and Robert were facing counts of first-degree murder in Dennis Strongquill's death. The Crown prosecutor in the case, Bob Morrison, believed that Laurie was as much involved in the killing as Sand, even if she hadn't fired a single shot. Under the Criminal Code of Canada, the murder of any peace officer, such as a police officer or corrections officer, is automatically first-degree murder, regardless of whether or not the murder was planned. The subsection of the law had been enacted in the 1970s when capital punishment was abolished in Canada.

Defence attorney Greg Brodsky, who was aided by Jason Miller, had worked on behalf of Paul Bernardo and was now working on behalf of Sand, and he dropped the first bombshell of the trial before it even began. He filed a motion with the court, arguing that the automatic first-degree murder charge for killing a police officer was unconstitutional. Brodsky argued in a brief that the life of a police officer has no higher value than any other human life. He cited the Canadian Charter of Rights and Freedoms sections that guaranteed the right to protection from arbitrary imprisonment and the right to fundamental justice in law.

The reaction to Brodsky's motion was swift and critical.

"Police in this country do not place their lives on a higher scale, but there is a huge distinction in that police officers place themselves in the line of fire in the course of duty and require more protection," said Grant Obst, president of the Canadian Police Association.

"It's a big slap in the face, but we're getting used to it," said Teresa Strongquill, the eldest of Dennis' six children.

The motion was nothing more than a waste of time. Judge John Menzies shot down the argument quickly. Menzies did rule, however, that neither Sand nor Bell would have to wear handcuffs during the trial, only leg shackles.

The trial officially began in April 2003. The jury consisted of seven women and five men, most of them elderly.

Morrison started off the trial in his opening remarks by reading excerpts from a diary Robert had kept during what had turned out to be a 10-day crime spree.

"Now, we've got so much firepower that if a cop pulls us over, he'll be one sorry mother f*****. And I feel so out of control, cuz I've set very few rules. So we can do whatever we wanted. We've got money, booze, drugs and I've got my two favourite people now. With me!"

The first few days of the trial were devoted to the stand-off at the Wolseley Motel, where Danny was killed. An audio-tape of police radio traffic during the confrontation was played for the jury, and the results of Danny Sand's autopsy revealed that the bullet had entered his right cheek and brain, killing him instantly. The autopsy also revealed that Danny had smoked marijuana anywhere from 12 minutes to four hours before the shooting. His body also bore another gunshot wound, consistent with the volley Auger had fired at the truck at the initial crime scene.

Officers who participated in the standoff at Wolseley were then called to testify. Brodsky went after each one, wondering why there was no attempt made to negotiate with the trio before giving the order to take out Danny Sand. Corporal Darren Topping said there was no time to call an experienced negotiator. He did admit that the officers on scene had bullhorns, but they weren't used.

"At that point in time I would have preferred to keep both hands on my rifle," Constable Murray Chamberlin retorted.

One officer repeated Robert's remarks about ruining his birthday, while another reported that at the time of Bell's arrest she had been wearing an "excessive amount of jewelry," which included 21 chains, bracelets and necklaces, three crosses, nine gold rings and three watches; all were traced back to a string of earlier break-ins. Police officers who searched the motel room and truck after the stand-off also found a DVD player and DVDs, two bottles of liquor, a baseball bat, knives, 10 rifles, over 1000 rounds of ammunition and a single stuffed teddy bear wearing a Santa hat.

The testimony that dragged on through April revealed that Strongquill's shooting had been the climax of a 10-day crime spree, starting in rural Alberta and ending at the motel. A litany of Crown witnesses told the court that Robert had left the Stan Daniels Healing Centre after meeting Laurie, determined to help get her off drugs but unable to do so because of the conditions of his parole. Danny had joined them, and the trio had decided to head east to start a new life, ideally somewhere on the coast, away from the long arm of the law.

The trio hitched a ride from Danny's roommate to Red Deer, where they stole a truck and headed to Laurie's hometown of Athabasca. From there they headed to Hondo, Alberta. They retraced their steps and dropped in on Sharon Ford, who lived near Westlock. She was the mother of a friend of Robert's who had died years earlier. Sharon and Laurie cut and bleached Robert's hair before the trio headed east. Along the way, they repeatedly ditched and torched their vehicles, stealing new ones in order to keep the police off their trail. In the town of Thorhild, Alberta, Danny and Robert robbed a branch of the Bank of Nova Scotia, but were forced to discard almost the entire $4000 when a dye pack exploded afterwards. They continued stealing vehicles and breaking into houses, helping themselves to whatever happened to be available, including firearms and ammunition.

Robert and Laurie had not been complete angels in custody after their arrest either. In 2002, both were involved in separate assault incidents. Robert, the Crown alleged, assaulted a prison guard in what the corrections authority deemed to be an escape attempt. Laurie had joined in on a group beating of a child abuser, pouring a cup of urine on top of the woman.

While the case against Robert seemed to be relatively tight, the first-degree murder charge against Laurie was less so. The defence argued that Bell was simply in the wrong place at the wrong time, in love with the wrong man. In order to prove first-degree murder, Morrison, who painted the pair as a modern-day Bonnie and Clyde, had to prove Bell was somehow involved in the killing. And he had an ace up his sleeve, albeit a questionable one.

Shortly after Bell's arrest, Rose Ferguson, 38, was lodged in cells with her. Rose had been arrested trying to return to Canada from the United States to care for her mother. She faced an outstanding charge of stabbing her common-law husband. After sharing a cell with Bell for a few days, Ferguson was released and the charge against her dropped.

She showed up in Brandon to testify for the Crown, where she said that Bell had opened up to her during their time together. Rose told the court that Bell had been laughing and joking about the murder, going so far as to say she had spurred Robert on by yelling, "Kill him, kill him!" during the shooting.

"She talked about what happened as if it was amusing, like a big joke. She didn't care that a person died. She wasn't sorry for what they did to that police officer," Rose testified.

Ferguson's testimony seemed in line with a standard "mug shot" taken hours after Laurie's arrest, in which Bell, her hair in pig tails, is seen smiling for the camera. The pictures were also shown to the court.

Rose, however, was not an ideal witness. She was, for starters, a jailhouse informant, and the use of informants normally carries a significant amount of risk because their motives and honesty often proves suspect. Judge Menzies was forced to warn the jury about Ferguson's testimony.

"The fact that she's a jailhouse informant should cause you some concern," he said.

The defence also targeted Ferguson's checkered history. Her criminal record dated back to 1985. She had an impaired driving conviction, she'd once left her child alone at home to go drinking, and she had allegedly stabbed her common-law husband. The latter charge, however, was dropped after she had been lodged with Bell. Ferguson denied any connection, stating that the charge was dropped because she was innocent.

In cross examination, Brian Midwinter, Laurie's lawyer, implied that Bell was only talking big because she was scared of Rose, who was the same height but 70 pounds heavier at the time. Morrison, however, was confident in Ferguson's testimony. Because she'd been in the U.S. when the killing took place, she hadn't heard about it or seen it in the papers. Ferguson also knew details that hadn't been disclosed to the press, and she hadn't gone to the police—they had come to her.

The defence didn't call any witnesses in either Robert or Laurie's defence. In his summation near the end of the trial, which had dragged on for almost 10 weeks, Crown prosecutor Morrison emphasized that neither Strongquill nor Auger could have predicted what would happen to them on December 20 and 21, 2001.

"They may as well have stopped at the gates of hell at that point," he told the jury. The Crown prosecutor pounded home the point that Strongquill was trapped inside the SUV when Sand fired the fatal shots.

"Sand could see Strongquill struggling like a caged animal and he hit him every time. There should not be one second's doubt that Robert Sand is guilty of first-degree murder."

Bell, Morrison argued, wasn't just along for the ride. She could have backed out of the crime spree at any time.

"She always knew, because of the arsenal of weapons, that as soon as a police officer stopped them, the police officer was probably going to die."

Brodsky offered a brief summation, arguing that Robert Sand should be found guilty of manslaughter because he was only trying to disable the police cruiser, not deliberately kill Dennis Strongquill.

The summations were due to wrap up on June 12. The court called a lunch break, where the jury was taken away for a bite to eat, and the rest of the court had time for a snack as well.

Suddenly, just as court was ready to reconvene, Sand leapt from the prisoner's box and fell on top of one of his own lawyers, Jason Miller. Pandemonium ensued as Robert jabbed a long, pointed thumbnail into Miller's throat, threatening to kill him. Laurie shrieked and jumped on top of one of the sheriffs heading for Robert, but she was quickly subdued and escorted from the room. Sand didn't have a chance. A swarm of sheriffs descended on him and pried him away from Miller. The judge was informed of what had happened, and Robert's hands were promptly hand-cuffed. The press reported a few days later that Sand had also been armed with a razor that he had lost in the struggle.

The most significant change that occurred after the incident was in how Laurie reacted when she returned to the court-room. She and Robert had been trying to maintain their relationship, trading notes in prison and chatting during court breaks. She now refused to even look at him.

Court was adjourned for the day. Midwinter completed his summation on June 13, arguing that Bell wasn't guilt of anything.

"The only thing Laurie Bell is guilty of is loving the wrong guy."

He also told the jury that Bell had no chance to escape from the Sand brothers. She had no money, no way to get home and, had she left without being harmed, would have been stranded in the middle of the country in the dead of winter.

After hearing Judge Menzie's charge, in which he laid out the pertinent points of law the jury had to keep in mind when deliberating on the fate of the accused, the jury retired to debate the case and decide on a verdict. It didn't take them long. At 6:00 PM, only hours after beginning their deliberations, the jury informed the judge they had reached verdicts for both.

Robert Sand gratefully accepted a dose of sedatives from the prison staff before returning to the courtroom. Bell still refused to look at him. At 7:00 PM the jury filed in. The first verdict was a no-brainer for anyone who had attended the trial—Robert Sand was guilty of first-degree murder. His body sagged visibly.

"Yes!" Teresa Strongquill shouted when she heard the verdict.

The clerk of the court read out the charge of first-degree murder against Laurie Bell.

"Not guilty," the foreman replied.

The clerk read out the charge of second-degree murder.

"Not guilty."

The final possibility—manslaughter—was read aloud.

"Guilty," the foreman announced.

Bell's case was put over two weeks for sentencing arguments. For Sand, there was no need for a hearing as the sentence was automatic—life in prison, with no possibility of parole for 25 years.

A victim impact statement, prepared by Strongquill's sister Ruby Brass, was submitted to the court.

"I will no longer be able to see my brother's smiling face, hear his laughter, feel his pain, hear him cry, hear him sing, hear his stories of his love for his children and feel the love that was there because he is gone.

"Dennis was a role model for the community and for his children. He was very proud to have worn the uniform of an RCMP officer. We are very proud of him. We were not ready for Dennis to leave us, it was too premature and unfair. He was proud to be a new father but now he will not be able to fulfill that role."

Menzies took dead aim at Sand as he passed sentence for his role in what the judge described as a "cowardly slaughter."

"You are not a stupid man. You are an intelligent man. The only conclusion I can come to is that you hate society. You can't tolerate authority. You hate the police. In your diary you said this was a war. But this wasn't war. It isn't war when only one side knows about it."

Sand was led from the room, to be housed in a cell while corrections officials prepared to transfer him to a maximum-security facility in Québec. Again, Bell refused to look at him.

Two weeks later, Bell was back in court, with her lawyer in tow. Midwinter assured Judge Menzies that Laurie no longer had any feelings for Sand because of his attack on his own lawyer. The Crown was asking for 10 years. On July 1, 2003, Laurie received exactly that, minus three years for the time she'd already spent in custody at a credit of two days for every one served.

"She's a parent's nightmare," Menzies said. "Her life has been plagued with drug addiction on the streets of Edmonton. It's not a happy life and it's not one that shows much hope."

∽

Months after his sentence, Sand was still making headlines.

While in custody in July 2003, he consented to media interviews, during which he played up his reputation as a bad ass. He claimed he'd never actually straightened out after his 1998 sentence, that he used all kinds of drugs in prison and in Stan Daniels, but he just knew how to beat the system.

He claimed that at the age of 14 he'd killed a drug dealer in self-defence. The RCMP in Alberta looked into the statement, but found no open cases in the time line Robert described.

In the end, Robert told the media he'd probably die in prison.

"I'm not a strong believer in suicide, but there are many ways a person could die in prison."

He offered little in the way of an apology for the murder of Dennis Strongquill.

"I have no sympathy for that uniform at all....From what I hear he was a decent man."

Sand's premonition that he would die in prison almost came true in May 2005. Three Native gang members, upset that Sand was bragging about shooting Strongquill, who had been Native as well, descended on Robert in the exercise yard, beating and stabbing him. Robert walked away, but the group pursued him and continued the assault. Two of the men were later convicted of assault and received four-month jail sentences.

Laurie's time behind bars has not been uneventful either. She appealed her conviction, but that was shot down. In 2006 she assaulted an inmate with a can of mushrooms. That same year, she was caught using morphine, blaming the use on the shootings of four Mounties in Mayerthorpe in 2005, which she said reminded her of her own crimes.

In March 2008, Laurie Bell was released from prison on statutory release, despite concerns about her chances of re-offending. The National Parole Board stated she was an "undue risk to commit a violent offence." One condition of her release is that she have no contact with Robert Sand. Her current whereabouts are not known.

~

From Dennis Strongquill's death came some advancements in officer safety from the RCMP. Even before the trial began, officers in Manitoba were informed that they were required to wear their bulletproof vests at all times, and every police vehicle was to be equipped with a shotgun. In 2003, the federal government followed suit, making body armour mandatory for all RCMP officers nationwide.

Chapter Two

Corporal James Galloway

Killed: *February 28, 2004, Spruce Grove, Alberta*
Suspect: *Martin Ostopovich—shot and killed
by police*
Status: *Case closed*

⁓

Cito stared back at the camera, as if someone had called his name.

The photograph of the German shepherd splashed across the newspapers around the Capital region, his muzzle greying with age, looking back over his shoulder towards the camera. Dogs can't cry, but they can express sorrow, and there was sadness imprinted on Cito's face. The image spoke for itself.

It's rare that dogs are allowed to attend funerals, but Cito was as much a member of the Galloway family as the veteran RCMP officer's own children. The dog, trained to spring into action on his master's command, was inside Sherwood Park Alliance Church in Sherwood Park, Alberta, a suburb southeast of Edmonton. As the service proceeded, Cito sighed and whined audibly, cracking the hearts of the nearly 4600 people who had come to say goodbye to Corporal Jim Galloway.

As a police dog, Cito was trained to attack suspects on command, to sniff out danger and to protect his master, as well as those his master wanted protected. He was an animal, but everyone in attendance could see by looking at Cito that he missed his master, just as much as everyone gathered in the church, if not more. In his own way, Cito was mourning the loss of his best friend.

Cito's loss had come a week before, in a confrontation that no one could have predicted and that no one had the power to stop.

February 28, 2004

The city of Spruce Grove, population 19,496, is one of Edmonton's "satellite communities." Located just a few kilometres west of the province's capital, the city ranks as Alberta's 11th largest in terms of population. Because of its small size, it does not merit a separate police force like those found in Edmonton, Calgary or Lethbridge. Subsequently, like every other municipality in Alberta, the RCMP is in charge of policing the tight-knit community.

From a policing standpoint, Saturday, February 28, 2004, had been a quiet one. It was a cold day for much of the central region of Alberta, especially in Spruce Grove. The mercury was threatening to plunge to –20°C. Early that afternoon, the entire atmosphere of the community changed drastically.

At approximately 1:00 PM, the Spruce Grove detachment of the RCMP received a phone call from a resident of Greystone Drive. The caller informed the police that he had gone outside and discovered a bullet hole in his vehicle, a rather chilling find to go along with the weather of the day. One officer was dispatched to the scene to investigate and was soon joined by a second constable. Both men knew the address of the complainant, and they also knew the person who lived next door.

The two officers examined the bullet hole in the vehicle then looked up to trace its trajectory. From the direction and the angle of impact, they discerned that the bullet had been fired from the house next door. That inference was further supported when they found that the screen covering the kitchen window of the home next door appeared to have a hole in it.

They carefully approached the front door of the complainant's next-door neighbour, well aware of who could potentially greet them. After a quick knock on the door by one officer, a woman pulled open the door and told the pair exactly what was going on, warning them against coming inside. When asked if she would like to come with them, the woman quickly agreed.

Wendy Ostopovich accompanied the two officers to the nearby police vehicle, where she began to tell the story of her last 24 hours. The man inside her home was her husband, Martin Ostopovich, a person well known to both the police and the community at large.

Up until 1999, Martin Ostopovich was considered a jack-of-all-trades who could fix a car, renovate a house or smith a gun. He was one of eight children, born with a fraternal twin named Marv. Their father was a career police officer in Windsor, Ontario. Martin's childhood had been far from happy. His father ran the household with strict military precision. Marv said violations of house rules were punished severely, usually with beatings.

Martin dropped out of school sometime around Grade 9 or 10, Marv later recalled, and at the age of 16, decided to head west to Alberta for work. He took whatever work he could find, driving trucks or working construction.

"He could build his own guns. He could take anything apart. He was very mechanically inclined," Marv later said.

Along the way Martin married Wendy, and the couple had two children—a son, Martin Jr., and a daughter Jennifer. For the most part, Ostopovich was remembered as a kind man who helped out his neighbours whenever he could, going so far as to repair their cars. He and Wendy enjoyed camping and fishing in the Rocky Mountain Foothills. Ostopovich was also a skilled gunsmith, and other hunters often brought him their guns for repair.

Then, in 1999, Ostopovich was involved in a serious vehicular accident in Yukon. According to an interview with his mother-in-law, Shirley Eldon, Ostopovich had been driving a truck that rolled five times. As a result of the crash, Ostopovich suffered severe head trauma. Eldon said that the doctors had to stitch the back of his head together. Ostopovich survived the ordeal, but almost from the moment he woke up, he was a changed man.

Shortly after his discharge from hospital, Ostopovich started hearing voices. Eldon said he would "blurt out things that the voices were telling him." Sometimes those voices told him to kill people, but he resisted. He became convinced the police or the government had planted electronic bugs in his body, as well as a camera in his eye. On one occasion, he even took a knife to his neck to try to cut out one of the government implants. The subsequent wound, however, was minor. His general practitioner, Dr. Jeffrey Moss, went so far as to take x-rays of Ostopovich's body to show him that there were no foreign objects inside. Ostopovich rejected the x-rays' results.

He was also starting to reject the legal system. He had racked up a minor criminal record, including convictions for assault causing bodily harm, uttering threats, unsafe storage of a firearm and possession of a prohibited weapon. Just months before the February 28, 2004, incident, Ostopovich called the Spruce Grove detachment, saying that he was coming down to the building and was going to start shooting police officers. Constable Paul White, a member of the detachment and an Emergency Response Team sniper, waited for hours for Ostopovich to show up, but he never arrived.

It was clear there was little doctors could do to help Ostopovich. His symptoms were beginning to parallel those found in patients diagnosed with paranoid schizophrenia, a psychotic condition in which patients claim to hear things no one else can and who believe they are somehow being persecuted or watched. Along with the bugs in his body and the camera implanted in his eye, Ostopovich also believed that radio stations were talking to him. His behaviour was growing increasingly erratic and starting to alarm both Wendy and the children. Unfortunately, the family had few options available to them at that time. The only recourse they found was a section of the *Mental Health Act* that allows the police, if they believe an individual is a threat to either themselves or the public, to make an arrest and take the person to the nearest psychiatric facility for an assessment. From there, it is up to the psychiatric team evaluating the individual to decide whether or not the individual warrants intensive treatment. If the team considers the person to be a risk, they can order the patient held against their will for a specific time period, usually 30 days.

But in most cases, as White later indicated, the patients simply promise the psychiatric team that they won't hurt themselves or others, and they are set free before the 30 days elapse. General practitioners aren't usually notified about proposed courses of treatment, and the patient's progress is not followed up, otherwise known as a community treatment order.

By May 25, 2002, Wendy had no other options. She snuck away from her home and went to the Spruce Grove detachment, explaining her situation to the officers on duty. Under the *Mental Health Act*, they went to the house and took Ostopovich into custody before transporting him to the psychiatric ward at the Royal Alexandra Hospital in Edmonton. During the process, they also seized guns from the residence.

Upon admission, Ostopovich was immediately committed to a 30-day involuntary stay by doctors on the ward, who concluded that the 39-year-old was a danger to himself or others. Dr. Sandi Frank, who treated Ostopovich, documented that Martin said he was being persecuted by the police, whom he said he would kill. He also believed he had broadcasting implants inside his head. The doctors performed a CAT scan to show him there was nothing implanted in his brain. Much like the x-rays his general practitioner had performed, Ostopovich didn't believe the results.

Depending on which testimony or report you read, Ostopovich suffered from a paranoid psychosis, was paranoid-delusional or was a paranoid schizophrenic. Regardless of which diagnosis is true, the outcome was the same—Ostopovich thought both the police and government were persecuting him.

The medical team treating Ostopovich prescribed him medications and began working with him during his stay at the Royal Alexandra Hospital, during which time, according to Dr. Frank, Ostopovich made some improvements. He eventually admitted that he was wrong to threaten the police and that any complaint or grievance he had would be best pursued through legal channels. Despite Ostopovich's change in attitude, Dr. Frank still wanted Ostopovich to stay for a little while longer for further treatment. But on June 9, 2002, barely two weeks into his 30-day stay, Ostopovich checked himself out of the hospital and went home, against the doctors' wishes, surprising Wendy when he returned. He made no secret that he was unhappy about what she had done.

For the first two months at home, Ostopovich seemed to level out. He took his medication as prescribed, and the symptoms of his mental illness abated somewhat. The medication, however, wasn't all covered by insurance, meaning the family often had to fork out as much as $300 per month for his drugs. He took his drugs sporadically, and his behaviour subsequently seesawed between normal and the state he had been in when first admitted to hospital. In 2003, a frustrated and scared Wendy left Martin until he promised to start taking his medication again. She returned after one month. Later that year, Ostopovich again stopped taking his medication.

It was a problem for which there was no tangible solution. Alberta, unlike other provinces, didn't have community treatment orders in which patients were checked on and where those who weren't taking their medications were returned into involuntary custody. There was little Wendy could do to convince her husband to comply with his doctors' orders when he had so many other voices in his head competing for his attention.

On the evening of February 27, 2004, Wendy came home late to find Martin drinking a bottle of rye and listening to loud music. He was hearing voices again. There was blood on his hands, and he kept yelling at Wendy, calling her names. She was so scared that she left the home and spent the night sleeping in her car outside an arena in Spruce Grove. When she came back in the morning, Martin was asleep on the couch. He awoke around noon, visibly aggravated, mumbling to himself. He told Wendy that the voices were talking to him again, and they were telling him to kill someone. At that point, he formed his hand into the shape of a gun and pointed it at her.

Shortly afterwards there was a knock at the door. Martin told Wendy to go and answer the door. As she did so, he started making his way towards the bedroom where he kept two high-powered rifles.

In the police car, Wendy told the two officers that the front door was the only exit, and that Martin didn't have access to a police scanner. The pair had already radioed in to the detachment to the senior officer on duty, Sergeant Peter Koersvelt, who responded along with another constable. When the sergeant arrived, Wendy informed him of her husband's mental status, stating he was "paranoid delusional" and that he had not been taking his medication as prescribed.

The group on scene decided to remove Wendy from the area, taking her to the detachment. Shortly afterwards, the officers learned that Ostopovich had been making telephone calls—to the media. Martin had called the local CTV affiliate CFRN and told the person on the other end of the line that "someone was going to die today."

More officers descended on the scene, setting up a border around the cul-de-sac. Koersvelt slowly drove around the area, double-checking the perimeter and trying to take in as much information as he could. He later testified that as he passed in front of the Ostopovich home, he could see Martin moving around in the kitchen. He also said he could see a "black tube" sticking out of the same damaged window that the first two officers had noted when they arrived on scene. At that point, the sergeant ordered that every nearby resident be contacted by phone and told to remain in their basements until the danger had passed.

Then Koersvelt got a call. Central telecommunications (telecoms) received a phone call from someone claiming to be Martin Ostopovich. Koersvelt asked for the call to be put through to his cell phone, and he tried to engage Ostopovich in conversation. Ostopovich, however, wasn't listening. After referring to Koersvelt as a "f****** rat," he demanded to know why they had taken his wife away. Despite Koersvelt's efforts to calm him down, Ostopovich informed the sergeant that he was going to "take out" the next person he saw, regardless of whether that person was a civilian or a police officer. Martin then promptly hung up.

Koersvelt stashed his cell phone and picked up his radio. The situation was escalating, and he knew he needed additional help. After calling for more officers to help secure the area, Koersvelt put in a call requesting the assistance of the Emergency Response Team (ERT).

~

In everyday vernacular, the public refers to specialized police assault teams as SWAT teams, standing for Special Weapons And Tactics. An RCMP ERT is exactly the same as a SWAT team—their members consist of highly trained police officers, proficient in marksmanship and assault tactics, whose job is to deal with dangerous situations and bring them to an end, preferably peacefully. Each ERT consists of 12 members—one team leader, who directs the officers under his command; three snipers, who deploy around the area of concern and act both as the eyes and ears of the ERT, as well as provide a long-range cover fire option; and eight assaulters, officers who are trained in the use of submachine guns, shotguns, less lethal munitions and different devices such as flash-bang grenades. The job of these latter officers, as their title describes, is to assault whatever target the police are focused on, whether it be a building, a vehicle or an airplane. Heavy body armour, automatic weapons and diversionary devices are on hand in case a confrontation escalates to a life-threatening situation.

Although the officers who make up an ERT are among the most physically fit and highly trained officers, in Alberta, they do not operate as a full-time unit. ERT members are RCMP officers assigned to other detachments in the area, performing regular policing duties. They are called out when a detachment requests assistance. On average, an ERT trains together twice a month. Their special skills and tactics are seldom needed, but they are ready to respond whenever their presence is demanded.

In this case, the leader of the ERT for the area radioed in that a call for their assistance had been received and that the team would likely arrive at the location at around 4:00 PM. In the meantime, Koersvelt called telecoms back and ordered the Ostopovich phone line locked down so that he could only contact the police.

Koersvelt kept watch on Ostopovich's home. The man wasn't sitting idle. Koersvelt could plainly see him moving around the home and watched nervously as Ostopovich twice left the house: once to put something in the garbage and a second time to go to his truck. Each time, he promptly returned inside. In between, Ostopovich continued to make abusive phone calls to telecoms, threatening to come down to the detachment and shoot it out with the officers there.

At approximately 3:55 PM, Koersvelt decided to try to talk to Martin again. This time the conversation lasted approximately 25 minutes, but Koersvelt made no more headway in talking Martin down. He was agitated and growing increasingly irrational. Martin asked to speak to his wife, "to say goodbye," and repeated his threats to leave the home and drive down to the detachment. He called Koersvelt a liar and said that he was "going to take the war to you." His outbursts became more disjointed and aggressive, going so far as to declare that the Hells Angels were working for the police, and that he was determined "to hurt someone before he goes." Ostopovich became so worked up during the phone conversation that Koersvelt, standing a block away, could clearly hear Martin yelling without using his cell phone. Just as the RCMP hostage negotiators showed up on scene, Ostopovich hung up again.

The arrival of the two negotiators also heralded the arrival of the ERT. Along with the negotiators, team leader, snipers and assaulters, the members of the unit were also joined by a police dog handler. The RCMP had decided to embed dog handlers within ERTs, in case a suspect needed to be tracked or taken down.

In this case, the dog handler was a familiar face, even though he worked in Sherwood Park. Almost every RCMP officer in the Capital region knew Corporal "Screamin' Jim" Galloway.

~

In the dog-handling community of the RCMP, 55-year-old Galloway was practically a legend. The 32-year veteran of the RCMP had been around dogs and policing for most of his life. He could have retired years ago.

"But that's not how Jim was," said Assistant Commissioner Bill Sweeney, the senior officer for all RCMP units in Alberta and a friend of Galloway's. "He was an incredible guy."

Born in 1948 in Montréal, James Wilbert Gregson Galloway spent practically his entire life surrounded by dogs. His father Duncan raised beagles and retrievers, which meant that James was around them constantly. It was also Duncan who encouraged his son to join the RCMP, which he did in 1969. After finishing his training, the young constable was posted to Ottawa and worked security detail at Rideau Hall, the residence of Canada's governor general.

From there he moved on to work in Elbow, Saskatchewan, and then to Swift Current. In 1972, he married his high school sweetheart Margaret. The couple had three children—Jason, Karen and Cory—as well as eight grandchildren.

In 1975, Galloway's love of policing and dogs finally had a chance to intersect. His request to transfer to the Police Dog Service Training Centre in Innisfail, Alberta, was approved, and Galloway officially began training as a police dog handler. Over the course of his career, he had five "partners"—Kayla, Shep, Max, Danko and Cito. Each dog was trained to track, search for and subdue suspects, as well as to help find lost people. All of Galloway's dogs were also trained to sniff out illegal drugs.

After a brief stint in Montréal at Dorval Airport, Galloway was posted to Fort Saskatchewan in 1977, a small city on Edmonton's outskirts. He never left the province of Alberta again. He soon became a legend in the policing community, not only for his dedication to his work, but also for the extra hours he spent working with civilians, training dog owners to assist with search and rescue duties.

In addition, Galloway had the questionable honour of helping transport convicted American serial killer Charles Ng back to the United States. Ng and partner Leonard Lake were responsible for the murders of at least 12, but as many as 25 people at Lake's California ranch. When the police came looking for him, Ng managed to flee across the border to Calgary, Alberta, where he was later taken into custody for resisting arrest while shoplifting from an outlet of The Bay on July 6, 1985. When two officers confronted Ng, he pulled out a gun and shot one of the officers in the hand. The officers were still able to overpower the serial killer, who was later sentenced to four-and-a-half years in a Canadian prison. After a lengthy extradition battle with the United States, on September 26, 1991, Ng was finally returned to American authorities, with Galloway assisting in the prisoner transfer.

To everyone around him, Galloway was known as "Screamin' Jim."

"Everywhere he went he was a million miles an hour. That was his style," said Corporal Judi Watt, a friend of Jim's for 13 years.

It was that style that made Galloway so good at his job. His time as a dog handler had been a storied one, as Galloway and whoever his canine partner was at the time continually used their skills to help the communities around them.

"Jim is one of the few people I could actually call a legend," said Sergeant Steve Marissink. "When you knew you were getting Jim Galloway for your dog man, you knew you were getting the best."

That legend grew from the number of rescues and captures Jim logged during his extensive career. Two such incidents in particular stand out.

In August 1996, an 83-year-old man became lost in the bushes near Faust, 310 kilometres north of Edmonton. William Courtoreille was a Native elder, as well as a healer, and had gone into the woods looking for specific herbs to help treat an eye infection that had left him blind in one eye and the other irritated. He went into the bush on August 16 and didn't return. His family started searching for him the following day, but found nothing.

"We thought something had happened, with his age, with that storm," said Courtoreille's son Roger, describing the thunderstorm that blew through the area overnight. "We figured maybe he'd fallen in the creek, or there was something with his heart. Anything could happen at that age, being in the bush that long."

William's family called the RCMP, who dispatched Galloway and then-partner Danko to the area to help find Courtoreille. Galloway and Danko boarded a flight for Faust shortly after noon that day in the company of four other civilian dog handlers and their dogs. Not long after takeoff, Galloway received some stressful news—not only was William still missing, but the RCMP in the area also reported that a fugitive had gone missing in the same area. Galloway was ordered to find the man before he started searching for Courtoreille.

Tracking the fugitive, as it turned out, was relatively simple. The RCMP had already received a tip that the man was hiding in a house in the area. When the police arrived, the man dashed out the backdoor in bare feet. Galloway and Danko took up the pursuit, with the German shepherd sniffing out the man's trail before finally locating him. When faced with the snarling police dog, the fugitive immediately surrendered.

With the first matter taken care of, Galloway rejoined the civilian search crew searching for Courtoreille. His family members were all called out of the woods, because their scent could distract the dogs. For Danko, however, the distraction was minimal. Within 30 minutes, Danko picked up a scent that led him directly to Courtoreille, who was drenched in rain and knee-deep in a bog. He was wet and cold, but he was still alive.

Best friend Garry Gerber, who flew to Faust to help Galloway out, observed his friend during the flight home.

"Jim wasn't one for saying how good he'd done. He didn't care if the media ever put him in the paper. But that particular day, he was pretty pumped. When you catch a bad guy and find a good guy within a couple of hours of each other, you know you did a good day's work."

Eight years later, Galloway was again called in to track a missing person under less-than-ideal circumstances. On the afternoon of February 11, 2004, a three-year-old boy named Tod was playing with his dog Scruffy in the backyard of his family's Lake Eden acreage under the watchful eye of his mother. Carol was baking cookies when Tod's sisters came home from school. She took her eyes off him for just a minute, and that was all it took for Tod to disappear. Carol and her girls searched everywhere, but couldn't find Tod, Scruffy or his sled. When Carol called her husband Garth in a panic, he immediately called the RCMP, who called in Galloway.

With night falling, the child was in danger. The mercury was plunging below −20°C, too cold for any toddler to be out in the wild alone, dog or no. Yet it wasn't Galloway's dog Cito who found the boy, but Galloway's own trained eye. Accompanied by Constable Travis Lindemann, Galloway slowly followed a set of tiny tracks in the snow that Lindemann couldn't even see.

"I was baffled at first," Lindemann said. "I thought he was wrong. I didn't see anything."

But Galloway kept following the tiny indents, apparently made by the side of a small boot. The officers waded two kilometres into the bush, the snow sometimes up to their hips, when they noticed something on a ridge. That something was Tod, who was cold and confused, and refused to come down when the officers called to him. But he still had his sled, and he still had Scruffy.

Galloway went to Tod, scooped the child up in his arms and started to carry him back, but he flagged down an officer searching the area on a snowmobile and handed Tod off. After returning to the family's home, Galloway didn't bother going inside. He just got into his truck and drove away.

"He didn't speak to the family or want any kind of pat on the back at all," Lindemann recalled.

It was for that kind of service and for his work with civilian search and rescue groups that Galloway was honoured in 2002 with the Queen Elizabeth II Golden Jubilee Medal, given to Canadians who have made outstanding contributions to their communities or the country as a whole. Galloway continued to train hard, dismissing the idea of retirement. And he had finally developed a new tool of sorts for the RCMP. He had trained his latest partner, 10-year-old German shepherd Cito, to sniff out cadavers, making Cito the only police dog in Canada capable of doing so.

Galloway was also regularly getting called out with ERTs, averaging approximately 20 call-outs per year. He'd told his wife Margaret that he had once been shot at during a call-out 15 years earlier, but that he was always extremely careful on the job. In fact, Galloway's colleagues said he was usually in the thick of the action, rather than confined to the sidelines. Safety was his priority—not only his own, but that of the other officers around him as well.

"He was not a cowboy," said Sergeant Steve Marissink. "In terms of officer safety, he was second-to-none."

On February 28, 2004, after doing some volunteer work, Jim Galloway was heading to his home in Sherwood Park when he received the call out to Spruce Grove. He called Margaret and told her he was heading out on a call with Cito. Galloway arrived on scene in his RCMP SUV, one of the largest vehicles available to the small army of police officers who was taking up residence on Greystone Drive.

The ERT members on scene were having problems deciding on the best way to set up around Ostopovich's house. With the neighbouring houses tucked in close to their target residence, Martin had a broad view of the entire cul-de-sac. That meant it was difficult to get the ERT assault teams in position without being seen and to get the snipers in a good spot.

In the end, the team was split into two, with assaulters stationed on the far side of the neighbouring houses. While it got them close to the house, neither team could actually see Ostopovich's front door. That meant the ERT had to rely on radio transmissions from the three snipers to stay informed. One sniper set up on the roof of the house behind Ostopovich's residence, while the other two, one of which was Constable Paul White, took their positions behind a fence in a yard across the street from the house.

The situation didn't allow the ERT officers to respond quickly. During one of two conversations with the unit's negotiators, Ostopovich talked about music; he had actually been able to go to his truck to retrieve a CD and return inside before anyone could take any action. Not only were the assaulters too far away and without a clear line of sight to the residence, but Ostopovich's truck also was parked close to the front door.

Based on Ostopovich's earlier threats—that he would drive to the detachment to shoot it out with the police—the members of the ERT were faced with the real possibility that Martin could try to leave. But the officers on scene had few ideas to prevent him from leaving. The way the truck was parked left only the rear tires exposed, meaning they could shoot them out, but that would only slow Ostopovich down, not stop him. Someone raised the idea of putting a few rounds through the truck's engine block, but that too was ruled out—they would need a sound-suppressed (silenced), high-powered rifle so that the sound of gunshots would not aggravate Ostopovich further. The ERT had such a weapon—a silenced .308 rifle—but it was in Regina for repairs.

If Martin got to the truck and tried to leave, the team suggested blocking the opening to the cul-de-sac. But the entrance to the cul-de-sac was so wide and broad that there was no way the officers could cut it off entirely. Given that Ostopovich could see almost everything they did, they also ruled out the suggestion of parking a cruiser behind his truck, afraid it might inflame the situation. The effect might also be minimal—Ostopovich's truck was a rugged 4 x 4 that could easily rip through the small fence it was facing, allowing Martin access to the alley.

Negotiations were getting nowhere. The officer talking to Ostopovich was unable to build any rapport with the increasingly agitated man. Besides talking about music, during which time Martin made his brief excursion outside, all the negotiator could do was listen to Ostopovich mutter more threats. Ostopovich used the expression "suicide by cop" in one conversation (generally denoting an individual who acts in an aggressive manner towards police in the hopes of being shot). Martin never once said that he was willing to walk away from the situation. His only request was to speak to his wife.

"He wanted to say goodbye," the negotiator later said. The team had no intention of allowing that to happen. If Ostopovich got the chance to say goodbye to his wife, it could propel him towards taking the next step—whether that meant taking his own life or shooting at police.

In the meantime, the ERT leader had devised a "desperation" plan in case Martin tried to leave. In conversations with other officers on the scene, team leader Constable Randy Pearson decided the only alternative was to use a police vehicle to ram Ostopovich's truck if he tried to drive off. If executed correctly, Pearson hoped the impact would stun Martin long enough for the assaulters to move in and yank him from his truck. The heaviest vehicle they had access to at that moment was Galloway's SUV. The ERT had never practiced the manoeuvre, but the officers felt it was their only option to prevent Ostopovich from leaving.

"I was comfortable as you can be ramming a vehicle with an armed man inside," Pearson later said. "How comfortable can anyone be with that?"

The next issue the unit needed to settle was who was going to perform the manoeuvre. One member volunteered, but Galloway immediately rejected that offer. He wanted to be the one behind the wheel. Pearson tried to talk him out of it, but Galloway refused. In the end, the plan was approved, with a little finessing. Galloway was paired with ERT Corporal Timothy Taniguchi, who would sit in the passenger's seat with his MP-5 submachine gun ready. Galloway and Taniguchi decided on their plan. There was some concern that the SUV's airbags might deploy on impact, but neither thought it detrimental enough to scrub the plan altogether. The two would wait until Ostopovich started backing out of the driveway, then Galloway would punch the gas and ram Martin's truck on the driver's side, effectively T-boning it. The pair hoped the combined weight and speed of Galloway's SUV would be enough to push the truck back or roll it onto its roof. After impact, both Galloway and Taniguchi would exit the SUV and take cover behind it. The police officers all agreed Ostopovich would be stunned, and it would be easy for the members of the ERT to move in and arrest him.

In all the planning for the manoeuvre, no one noticed there was no ambulance on scene.

The clock was starting to work against the RCMP. The time was fast approaching 6:00 PM, when the local evening news broadcasts would begin. CFRN had a news team nearby, waiting to deliver a live report. The negotiator, Constable David Wilkinson, began to worry that Ostopovich, who hadn't yet been told there was an ERT outside his house, might hear about it on the news, further escalating the situation. The team debated whether or not they should be the ones to tell Martin what was happening outside. Ultimately they decided the negotiator should be the one to tell him.

No one thought for a second to call CFRN to ask them to minimize their reporting, something news agencies have been willing to do in high-risk situations.

At 6:14 PM, the negotiator picked up the phone and called Martin. He informed him that there was an ERT outside the house.

"I don't think anyone expected the reaction we got that day," Wilkinson said later.

No sooner had Wilkinson informed Ostopovich about the ERT than Martin hung up the phone. The sniper on the roof promptly radioed in, informing the rest of the team that Ostopovich had exited the residence and was heading for the truck. He was also holding two rifles, one by the barrel.

With Ostopovich trying to get away, the ERT promptly put their desperation plan into action. As soon as Martin started backing his truck out of the driveway, Galloway floored the accelerator, aiming for the driver's side of the truck. Taniguchi later estimated that their speed at the time of impact was between 60 and 70 kilometres per hour. Moments later, the SUV slammed into the truck, exactly as planned. ERT member Constable Paul White later said he thought the manoeuvre had gone "beautifully."

But it hadn't. The team had hoped the force of impact would push Ostopovich's truck back or tip it over. Unfortunately, a row of parked cars on the far side of Martin's truck prevented this from happening. The impact, while forceful, didn't even jar Ostopovich's hands from the steering wheel.

"I distinctly remember the suspect, Ostopovich, turning in our direction. He stared right at me," Taniguchi said. "Then we struck the vehicle."

Galloway shifted the SUV into park, and both officers went for their doors. As soon as Taniguchi looked up, he saw Ostopovich grab one of his rifles and point it at him through the truck's open window. Instead of exiting the SUV as planned, Taniguchi ducked down below the dashboard, praying the engine block would provide sufficient cover. After a heartbeat, he rose up quickly and fired two rounds through the SUV's windshield towards Martin. Taniguchi immediately ducked back down, waited, then rose again and fired one more shot.

Taniguchi later said he knew Galloway had left the SUV per their earlier plan. He also testified he never heard Ostopovich fire a shot.

Taniguchi wasn't the only officer firing at Ostopovich. Members of the ERT, who were converging on the truck to arrest Martin, suddenly opened fire. It was later revealed that 12 rounds had struck Ostopovich. The severely wounded man was promptly disarmed and hauled from his truck onto the ground and handcuffed. Despite his injuries, no one bothered attending to him. Several officers later testified they saw Ostopovich lying on the ground bleeding, twitching and making "gurgling" noises. Everyone's attention was focused on the ground near the driver's side of Galloway's SUV.

"It was like watching a TV show," a neighbour, identified only as Jim, said afterwards. He claimed he heard upwards of 30 gunshots. One officer estimated the elapsed time from the negotiator's phone call to shots fired was no more than 20 seconds.

Constable Lori Blaylock was on the ground next to the dog handler's crumpled form, performing CPR. She initially thought that Galloway had suffered a heart attack. It was only when Galloway's body was turned over that they discovered he'd actually been shot. A single bullet had been fired the instant Galloway had stepped out of the SUV, entering his back. The effect was fatal—Corporal Jim Galloway died instantly.

It was only at that moment, as their comrade-in-arms lay dead on the ground, that Pearson realized no one had called in an ambulance to be on standby.

"It hit me at that point that we didn't have an ambulance on scene. It hit me like a hammer."

An ambulance was quickly dispatched to the scene, where paramedics were directed to Galloway's body. No one informed the responding team that there were actually two victims. Paramedics Chad Priche and Alan Hofsink both spent two minutes working on Galloway before anyone mentioned there was a second victim. Ostopovich was later rushed to hospital in Stony Plain, where he was pronounced dead.

The assistant chief medical examiner later confirmed that even if an ambulance had been on scene, both men still would have died. Galloway's wound was instantly fatal, while Ostopovich, suffering from 12 gunshot wounds, would have required surgical intervention and blood transfusions within 5 to 10 minutes of the shooting, neither of which paramedics are trained to do.

The standoff was over, but the outcome was far from what anyone had anticipated or wanted. The grief-stricken ERT members waved off investigators who were dispatched to the scene, claiming they were too emotional to talk. The team huddled up in private and discussed what had happened, which under normal circumstances would have been considered inappropriate and, in a trial scenario, highly prejudicial, the perception being the officers were trying to get their "stories straight." There was, however, not going to be a trial.

~

In Sherwood Park, Margaret had just finished making Jim's dinner when she heard the news report. Jim hadn't called. In the past, when discussing her fears about his deployments with ERTs, Galloway always told Margaret, "Don't worry about me because they won't phone you, they will come to the door."

At 7:30 PM the doorbell rang. When Margaret opened the door, she saw Bill Sweeney, an RCMP corporal, and a pastor standing on her doorstep. Their expressions were grim and sad. Margaret later said she didn't even have to ask why they were there.

The next day, members from surrounding detachments, as well as family and friends, descended on the Galloway home.

"I may not have told him that enough, but it's quite the thing to have a dad who was an RCMP member," said the Galloways' son Cory. "He always did the right thing."

The force, however, was slow in releasing details to the public about exactly what had happened. As a consequence, a rumour started to circulate around Ostopovich's neighbourhood that Galloway had actually been shot by another officer. That jolted the force out of its silence as they publicly denied the rumour. RCMP handguns are all 9 mm Special Edition Smith & Wesson, while their rifles and submachine guns fire 5.56-mm rounds. Although the force did not disclose the calibre of round that had killed Galloway, Margaret had already informed the press, from what she'd heard from the members on scene, that Jim was shot by a .303-calibre round.

Galloway's funeral was scheduled for Friday, March 5. The turnout was phenomenal, but Margaret felt it was appropriate. She said her husband had attended as many police funerals as possible during his career.

"And now it's his turn. And he deserves it," she said.

In total, 75 K-9 teams marched in a two-block procession, with Cito under the escort of one of Jim's colleagues, Sergeant Grant McCulloch. Some 2000 other officers attending the funeral marched as well, in bricks of 50. At one point during the procession, a photographer—who likely called out the dog's name to get his attention—snapped a heartbreaking picture of a mournful-looking Cito looking back at the camera.

"If we lost a dog in the line of duty, we'd have the same kind of feelings as what [Cito's] having now," said Lethbridge Police Service dogman Constable Brian Stef, who marched in the procession with his partner Zircon.

Throughout the march, Cito continued to look around.

"He gets confused when dad's not around," McCulloch later said.

Some 4600 mourners, including Cito, packed the Sherwood Park Alliance Church for the full regimental service, during which Galloway's best friend whimpered audibly.

The police dog's future was in doubt. Cito had spent a week living at the Edmonton police dog kennel while the rest of the Galloway family prepared for the funeral. Five days after the funeral, the RCMP announced that Cito had been retired from duty and was being sent to live with a longtime friend of the family, per Galloway's request.

While the force seemed to be doing its best to take care of Galloway's family in the aftermath of his death, it was revealed in November 2004 that Margaret had been left on the hook for $10,000 of Jim's full regimental funeral costs. Several other RCMP widows came forward with similar stories. The force responded with a statement explaining that they could only pay a certain amount as dictated by the federal treasury board. When the news broke, the Edmonton Police Association announced that it would cover the difference on Margaret's behalf. In the end it proved unnecessary—in January 2005 the RCMP reimbursed Margaret and one other widow for their husbands' funeral costs.

One month later, Red Deer County Council unanimously approved a recommendation to name a road outside Innisfail, near the Police Dog Training Centre, after Galloway.

∼

Whenever an individual dies because of the actions of police, whether in custody or during an altercation, Alberta's

Fatality Review Board, with the consent of the attorney general, is required to convene a fatality inquiry. Because Ostopovich died when the RCMP ERT opened fire on his vehicle, and an officer had died as well, an inquiry was automatic.

A fatality inquiry, typically presided over by a provincial court judge, is not a trial. Although witnesses do give testimony, evidence is presented and lawyers make arguments, the goal of the inquiry is not to assign blame but to deduce what went wrong and to use the findings to make recommendations as to how a similar situation could be avoided in the future.

Judge Peter Ayotte was appointed to preside over the inquiry into the deaths of Ostopovich and Galloway. The inquiry took place in Stony Plain, another satellite community only a few kilometres from Spruce Grove. The inquiry convened in November 2005 and sat a total of 13 days, ending in May 2006. Ayotte heard testimony from everyone involved in the case, including Wendy Ostopovich, the RCMP members on scene, doctors who had treated Martin Ostopovich in the past and the deputy chief medical examiner for the province. Lawyers representing both the Ostopovich and Galloway families, and one for the province, attended as well.

After hearing from several dozen witnesses, Ayotte issued his final report. He shied away from making any recommendations regarding the actual decisions the RCMP made that night, not wanting to "unduly shackle" them "with policies that neutralize their ability to adjust to the almost limitless scenarios they face." Instead, Ayotte issued 13 recommendations, ranging from the treatment of mentally ill individuals to how ERTs should be organized and what equipment they should have at their disposal.

In summary, Ayotte recommended that:

- the province fund a campaign to get more medical students into psychiatry

- special police mental health units be created to work in suburban areas

- in-patient facilities provide copies of their charts to the family doctor of a mentally ill patient

- the leader and second-in-command of an ERT become full-time positions

- the complement of part-time ERT members be gradually increased to 20 per team

- ERTs train for three days each month instead of two

- the province provide more mental health training for police negotiators

- the province provide extra funding to embed a paramedic with ERTs

- the RCMP maintain its current policy restricting the use of lethal force to situations in which an individual poses a threat to police or civilians

- the RCMP purchase an armoured personnel carrier (APC) to be used in high-risk situations

- the RCMP conduct an annual review of its equipment

- psychiatrists be allowed to hold an individual involuntarily for a minimum of 30 days, whether or not the symptoms that brought the individual into care have disappeared

- the province create legislation enacting community treatment orders

The province acted almost immediately on the recommendations that fell under its purview, drafting legislation in March 2007 allowing for community treatment orders.

"All we ever wanted was for Marty to receive the care he so desperately needed," the Ostopovich family later said.

The RCMP was supportive of most of Ayotte's recommendations but was restrained by finances. An APC, said one member, is "a very, very costly item," even though American SWAT teams have access to one or more per city. The Canadian Forces decided to step in and donated, not to the RCMP, but to the Edmonton Police Service, a retired 1978 Grizzly APC for that force's ERT. The Grizzly is also made available to the RCMP in the central and northern Alberta regions.

The Albert Solicitor General developed an online police course for police to educate them more about dealing with mental health issues.

The case is now considered closed.

Chapter Three

Constables Robin Cameron and Marc Bourdages

Killed: *July 7, 2006, Spiritwood, Saskatchewan*
Accused: *Curtis Alfred Dagenais*
Charges: *Two counts first-degree murder; one count attempted murder*
Status: *Trial begins September 15, 2008*

~

July 18, 2006

A farmer can find a lot of strange things in a field when he's out haying. There are plenty of animals, from groundhogs to snakes to rabbits and mice. Sometimes they're alive, and sometimes they're dead. There can be rocks that a farmer who's tilled his land for decades didn't know were there. Some landowners have even found unexploded training ordinance—bombs and artillery shells—left over from the days when a military base might have been stationed nearby, when troops practiced their skill from the ground or from the sky.

But seldom will farmers find a person in the middle of their field. On this day, that's exactly what Rosanne and Armand Smith found when they were out cutting down their summer crop of hay. They knew who the man was—everyone in the communities of Mildred or Spiritwood knew who he was, especially these days. And he was in pretty good shape, considering.

Neither Rosanna nor Armand knew what to do. Although they knew the man, who was basically using their land as a hiding place, they didn't really know him as a friend. He was more an acquaintance; one they'd prefer not to have.

But here he was, gingerly leaning on one foot, staring up at the Smiths as they approached him. In the middle of nowhere Saskatchewan, Rosanna and Armand did what farmers sometimes do best—they started to talk to him. And he started to talk back. As the morning sun rose into the afternoon, the man continued to talk, and the couple continued to listen. Before they knew it, three hours had passed. They should have been scared, even frightened, as many local area residents were these days, but rather than run away, they took the man into their home and served him up a cup of hot coffee. And he continued to talk.

Another three hours passed, and soon the man was all talked out. The story he'd told them was hair-raising, terrifying and infuriating, but the Smiths knew what they wanted out of him. When they first broached the subject, he refused, musing instead that it just might be better to kill himself. But as time wore on, the man seemed to finally come around. He rose from the table, hobbled his way towards the Smiths' vehicle and sat quietly as they drove into Spiritwood.

Shortly after 4:00 PM, Curtis Alfred Dagenais, who had been on the run for 11 days and was charged in the first-degree murders of two local RCMP officers, turned himself into police with no trouble whatsoever.

~

The town of Spiritwood, Saskatchewan, is a typical farming town. It has a small population, enough goods and services to supply the mostly farming folk who live on its perimeter and a main street that cuts right through the centre of town. It's also one of those towns where everybody knows everybody else. And knows their business.

Everyone knew Elsie and Arthur Dagenais. The couple had been married for 47 years, up until 2003. They had two children—a daughter named Grace, who had since married, and a son named Curtis, who hadn't. Arthur had a ranch just outside Mildred, a stone's throw from Spiritwood, where he leased out his lands to pasture.

But what had really caught the town's attention was that Elsie and Arthur no longer lived together. In fact, Elsie had moved out of the Dagenais farm in 2003 and now lived in a house on main street that she owned along with her 96-year-old mother, and Curtis, who was 41 years old. Elsie had been married to Arthur for almost 50 years, but she had left him, and divorce proceedings were underway.

Each side, of course, had their own story to tell. Elsie quietly told her friends of years of abuse at the hand of her husband, none of which were ever proven in any court. The one time Elsie had gone to court and filed a private prosecution against Arthur for sexual assault, the Crown prosecutor had decided to stay the charge, meaning that nothing happened.

The ranch was the family's biggest asset, and the division of marital property was at the centre of the divorce proceedings. According to Arthur, the family had already bailed Grace out once, cashing in their life savings to the tune of $384,000 to help their daughter and her husband get back on their feet. From his perspective, Grace had basically used up any inheritance she had coming. At the age of 69, Arthur knew his best days were behind him, and he wanted the farm, along with all of the machinery on it, to go to only one person—Curtis.

Elsie, of course, disputed the claim in divorce proceedings, arguing that she was entitled to 50 percent of the matrimonial assets, including the farm. The land and everything on it was valued at approximately $590,000. Whether she farmed the land or not was immaterial—Elsie wanted her half of the farm.

On July 7, 2006, Elsie made her wishes known to Arthur. Feeling his son was entitled to a warning, Arthur called Curtis to let him know that he probably wasn't going to get the whole farm, after all.

No one, not even Arthur himself, could have predicted what would happen next.

∽

Like the town in which it resides, the Spiritwood RCMP detachment isn't large. A handful of dedicated police officers, each with different levels of experience, patrol the town and the surrounding area as best as their resources allow. There was little in the way of major crimes—thefts and vandalism seemed to be the run-of-the-mill type of day for the officers posted there.

But working in a small town has its benefits—you get to know everyone, either through community programming and policing or by arresting the same individuals repeatedly. In the backwater of any small town, there are those who don't believe in the police, who see them as a government arm trying to oppress honest citizens who are just going about life as they see fit. Arthur Dagenais was one of those people. And he had instilled the same kind of paranoia into his son Curtis.

"Art has no respect for the police, and he drilled that into his son," one resident said.

On July 7, 2006, shortly after 9:00 PM, the Spiritwood detachment received a call of an assault complaint at a residence in town. A vehicle was dispatched to investigate the complaint. The two officers working that night were Constables Robin Cameron and Marc Bourdages.

The two men were a good match as far as police officers go. Each had more than five years experience in policing, and each had family who lived in the area or at least nearby. Bourdages had been stationed in Lac La Biche, Alberta, a small northern town that is dominated by Aboriginal people. He was born in Montréal but grew up in St. Eustache and Deux Montagnes in Québec. He'd joined the force as a highly prized candidate—intelligent, outgoing and bilingual. Lac La Biche was his first posting. During his time there, another police officer by the name of Natasha Szpakowski came to town to visit one of Marc's co-workers, who had been a member of her troop in Depot in Regina. When Marc and Natasha met, the chemistry was instant. Unfortunately for the couple, Natasha was stationed in Saskatchewan. A long-distance relationship ensued that burned up the phone lines until the pair finally married at the chapel at Depot in August 2003. They both accepted postings to Pelican Narrows so they could be together, and in March 2006, transferred to the Spiritwood detachment. In the winter of 2005, Natasha gave birth to their first child, a son named Luca, who was now nine months old.

Constable Robin Cameron's life had been a little more difficult than Bourdages, but she was equally respected in the community, if not more so. Born on the Beardy's Okemasis First Nation northeast of Regina, the 29-year-old was a perfect fit for community policing in a province where people of First Nations descent make up a significant part of the population. Robin had by no means led a perfect life, having dropped out of high school when she became pregnant. But she persevered and completed her Depot training, all the while devoting her free time to raising her daughter Shayne, now 11 years old. She also had a brother, crippled in a car accident when Robin was 12, who now lived in an assisted care facility.

"Robin is a very sweet and dedicated young girl," her uncle Ernie Cameron said. "Whenever she is around for family get-togethers she is always very jolly."

Cameron and Bourdages got the call about the assault complaint and headed towards the address, both groaning inwardly. The address was that of Elsie Dagenais. And according to initial reports, Curtis was somehow involved. Every single officer on the force knew about Curtis, so it came as no surprise when Cameron and Bourdages received new information that Curtis had allegedly called the RCMP earlier that evening to help remove someone from his property, a request the RCMP declined. Arthur had called as well, suggesting that the police attend the property.

When Cameron and Bourdages arrived at Elsie's property—which Curtis also owned—they found him involved in a verbal scuffle with both his mother and his sister Grace. According to reports taken at the scene, Curtis allegedly hurled Grace across the front of a car into the street during the argument. Cameron and Bourdages approached the situation as calmly as they could, trying to talk Curtis down and get him to back away. Their efforts, however, were rebuffed. Acting on the only information they had, Cameron approached Curtis and informed him that he was under arrest for assault.

Instead of complying with her instructions, Curtis dashed away from the officers, hopped into the cab of his truck and roared off into the night. Bourdages and Cameron jumped into their police cruiser to follow, radioing in that they were engaging in a pursuit. Another officer also radioed in that she was nearby and would help the pair.

The chase was on.

~

A criminal pursuit through the backwater roads of rural Saskatchewan looks nothing like the high-speed chases typical of larger urban areas. There are potholes, frost heaves and gravel to contend with.

The truck's tires kicked up clouds of dust as it weaved along rural roads for about 15 kilometres, heading in the direction of Mildred. Not just one but two police cruisers were now in pursuit, their overhead emergency lights flashing.

The officer in the second cruiser—Constable Michelle Knopp—followed Bourdages and Cameron as the chase wore on. Without any warning whatsoever, the truck ahead lurched to a stop. Bourdages and Cameron tried to stop but made contact with the truck. Knopp slammed on the brakes and opened her car door.

Three bangs pierced the night, jolting Knopp into a defensive position. She shielded herself behind the driver's side door of her cruiser and drew her 9 mm Smith & Wesson sidearm from its holster. In the glare of the headlights, she could see a man with a long gun struggling to get out of the driver's side of the truck. Recognizing that the booming shots had likely come from the long gun he was holding and not from either Bourdages' or Cameron's sidearm, Knopp wasted no time in acting. As the man started to make his way into the bush, Knopp pulled the trigger, firing multiple rounds in the direction of the suspect. Temporarily blinded by the muzzle flash of her weapon, Knopp blinked and surveyed the scene in front of her. The man she had been firing at had disappeared.

Her gun at the ready, Knopp moved slowly forward, wanting to check on Bourdages and Cameron while protecting herself from another attack. When she reached the side of the first cruiser and looked inside, all pretence of self-defence fell away. The airbags inside the cruiser had deployed. The windshield sported three holes, with cascading spider webs of cracked glass spread across its surface. And both Bourdages and Cameron had been hit.

More shocking still, both officers had been shot in the head.

Knopp pulled her radio to her lips and called in the shooting, as well as calling for an ambulance. At 10:24 PM, emergency workers arrived on scene, scooped Bourdages and Cameron from the vehicle into an ambulance and roared off, lights and sirens blazing. Both were still alive, but the nature of their wounds required immediate medical intervention. Bourdages and Cameron were transferred 150 kilometres south to Saskatoon, where they underwent surgery.

By the time the town awoke the following morning, news of the shooting had spread. Media descended on the scene, demanding answers. The killing of four RCMP officers in Mayerthorpe a year earlier still lingered heavily in the minds of both the force and the public. In this case, however, the suspect was nowhere to be found.

At least the Mounties knew who they were looking for.

⌥

There was little good news over the next two days unless you looked hard for it. Although Cameron and Bourdages had not yet been identified to the media, the force said that two officers had emerged from surgery at Royal University Hospital in Saskatoon.

"They're recovering, but it's really a wait-and-see kind of thing. Those first few hours are very important," Corporal Keith Bott told the media.

The facts as known were released to the press—that two officers had attended a residence on an assault complaint, and that the suspect had fled from police in a truck. Approximately 12 kilometres from Mildred, "all vehicles stopped and gunfire erupted," according to RCMP spokesperson Heather Russell. The two officers had sustained "very serious gunshot wounds," though no one would say where the bullet wounds were on their bodies. A third officer on scene had fired on the suspect, who had fled into the bush on foot. It was not known if she had hit the suspect. A long-barrelled gun had allegedly been used in the shooting.

In the minds of the RCMP, there were no doubts about who they were looking for, based on the evidence and reports they had on hand. By Saturday, July 8, dog teams, the Emergency Response Team and officers from nearby detachments were searching the bush for Curtis Alfred Dagenais, 41, of Mildred, Saskatchewan. The RCMP issued a description of Dagenais as a Caucasian male, 5 feet, 11 inches tall, weighing 158 pounds, with brown hair and green eyes. The suspect was last seen wearing blue jean cut-off shorts, a short-sleeved shirt and a baseball cap.

He was also considered to be armed and dangerous.

As many as 40 police cruisers descended on the region the following day as the officers on hand marshalled a search for their suspect. Based on the information at hand, the members in charge of the search cordoned off an area approximately 208 square kilometres in size from just south of Mildred to Larson Lake, south of Highway 12.

The people of Spiritwood were shocked at what had happened but weren't surprised when informed who the police were looking for.

"It's like another Mayerthorpe. But you never expect it to happen to you," one local resident told the press.

Many in the community were already starting to draw comparisons between Dagenais and James Roszko, the

Mayerthorpe resident who had gunned down four RCMP officers in 2005 before killing himself.

Another resident said that Curtis was "just weird."

∽

Curtis Alfred Dagenais had spent his entire life in Mildred, Saskatchewan. He was known throughout the community as a loner with few friends, with knowledge of the surrounding land and a palpable hatred and distrust of the police.

Few details of his childhood are available, though one court document alleges he was subject to frequent abuse at the hands of his father. Dagenais dropped out of high school and decided to head west to Lloydminster, that strange border town where a person living on the Saskatchewan side pays less vehicle insurance than someone living on the Alberta side. He worked on the oil rigs before finding work as a truck driver. It was in this profession that Dagenais' hatred of authority further crystallized.

The highway patrol officers in Saskatchewan soon became familiar with Curtis Dagenais. The government of Saskatchewan employs unarmed highway patrol officers to do exactly what their job title implies—patrol the highways. They have a radio, wear bulletproof vests and carry pepper spray, and they are responsible for one of the most dangerous operations any peace officer faces—a traffic stop. A driver might be pulled over for speeding, but officers have no way of knowing what awaits them when they approach the vehicle.

In his job as a truck driver, Curtis was often stopped for speeding. He was twice cited for carrying loads that exceeded weight or dimension regulations. Rather than change his behaviour to follow the rules, Dagenais went on the offensive. When officers pulled him over, he swore at them. He left threatening phone messages at weigh stations, and on one occasion, he actually followed a highway patrol officer home.

Eventually, his actions caught the attention of the judicial system. In November 1999, Dagenais was convicted of threatening to cause death to a highway traffic officer. In October 2000, he was convicted again, this time of uttering threats to cause serious harm to a highway patrol officer. Four years later, in August 2004, Dagenais was convicted on one count of assaulting a highway patrol officer, the same officer whom he'd been convicted of threatening in 1999. He was also convicted of one count of wilful obstruction for "operating a semi-tractor unit and trailer on a highway when seized under the Saskatchewan *Highway Traffic Act.*"

The union responsible for the highway patrol officers cited Dagenais' behaviour as a reason to ask the government for permission for their officers to carry guns. The union also petitioned the government to have Dagenais' name added to the Canadian Police Information Centre (CPIC) database as a violent person. The request was originally denied. A consultant hired by the government produced a report saying that while highway patrol officers wanted guns, they really didn't need them. Their request for firearms was denied.

In 2005, however, the union won a small victory when Dagenais was finally listed in CPIC as a violent person, which one officer later contended is "not something that's done lightly." That meant that any officer who stopped Dagenais and called in his name would receive a warning that he was known to be violent.

It was also known that Curtis had tried to kill himself in 2003. Emergency responders had been sent out to a lake and found the tip of a boat sticking out of the water's surface. They searched the area and eventually found Curtis on the opposite shore, cold and wet and injured—he'd beaten himself with a fishing rod.

Curtis returned to Mildred for good in 2004, operating a trucking business with his father as well as tending to the family farm, which he believed would eventually be turned over to him.

Despite Curtis' record of violent behaviour, according to lifetime friend Rick Lavoie who had known Curtis since kindergarten, he was incapable of killing the smallest animal.

"He didn't like killing anything. He couldn't stand the sight of blood."

Nonetheless, Lavoie did confirm that Dagenais was an experienced shooter, preferring to use a .308 rifle.

"Some people might not think he was that good of a guy, but you know what? All of us have our secrets, but I guess he has some deeper than I ever really thought."

∾

Fear was rampant in Spiritwood and Mildred, despite the growing number of police officers descending on the area. Officers from detachments across Saskatchewan, as well as from Alberta, made the trip to help assist in the search. They set up roadblocks all around Mildred, and officers asked drivers to open their trunks and truck drivers to allow inspection of their cargo, looking for any sign their suspect might be trying to make a getaway. Members of the Emergency Response Team, decked out in full camouflage and face paint, combed the search zone quietly and carefully, looking for footprints, broken tree branches and any sign that someone might have fled through the area. They knocked on farmhouse doors and searched grain bins, tractors and abandoned farm buildings.

Overhead, spotter planes criss-crossed the land and were joined by an RCMP search helicopter. Spotters with binoculars examined every square metre of land in front of them, looking for any sign of their wanted man. A no-fly zone was established, requiring other pilots to reroute around that airspace. The search, however, was unsuccessful. The dense brush and tall grass hindered the search team's efforts. Nevertheless, the RCMP was confident someone would find Dagenais soon. After all, he had fled into the bush in nothing more than a T-shirt and shorts.

Although it was summer and the evenings were warm, Curtis, they believed, was ill-equipped to last in the wild for too long, especially with his picture broadcast to every police agency and media outlet nationwide.

"There are only four people who know exactly what happened that night. Two are recovering from surgery, one of them we are still looking for, and the fourth, well, we don't know when [Knopp will] be able to talk," said one RCMP spokesperson when asked about the progress of the investigation.

The updates on Bourdages' and Cameron's condition were infrequent but usually repeated the same information— their condition was serious. Their families were at their bedsides, praying for their recovery.

There was one announcement that shocked some, but didn't surprise many others in the community. On Saturday, July 8, the RCMP announced that they had arrested Arthur Dagenais, 69, in Mildred and placed him in custody on charges of obstruction of justice and possession of an unregistered firearm. A justice of the peace ordered the elderly man held in custody until a court appearance on Tuesday morning in North Battleford.

As the search progressed, more and more information about Curtis and the events that may have provoked his alleged actions came to light. Lavoie, who had already described his friendship with Dagenais, stated that, during the chase, Dagenais had allegedly called a friend to meet him on the road to

Mildred, where he planned to stop. Lavoie declined to say who the friend was or how he knew about the plan, only saying that Dagenais simply wanted witnesses present when the police took him into custody. That friend never showed up, and the pursuit continued.

Relatives of Curtis also started talking, specifically his uncle, Herb Jaster, who explained what started the sequence of events on Friday night, as he'd heard them. According to Jaster, Arthur had allegedly phoned Curtis to let him know that, as a result of the divorce proceedings, Curtis likely wouldn't be receiving the entire farm, as Arthur had promised him.

"That just set him off. That's what started this episode here," said Jaster. "He hates everybody. He hates the police."

Jaster also explained that police in the area often checked up on Curtis with no warning.

"He resented that," said Jaster, who also added that the police asked him to leave his home for safety reasons, but he refused to do so.

"I just turned all the lights off, loaded the gun. That was [Friday] night and I'm still in the house, I haven't went out, and my gun is laying right here beside me."

Elsie Dagenais and her family also issued a statement, thanking the RCMP for their protection and extending their thoughts and prayers to the two police officers in hospital and their families.

Little had changed for Cameron and Bourdages. Their conditions were still described as "critical and tenuous." RCMP Commissioner Giulian Zaccardelli visited the town, stating the shootings were "the random acts of a madman." He also spent time visiting with the Cameron and Bourdages families at Royal University Hospital in Saskatoon. The visit from the RCMP's top cop added even more pressure on search teams to track down their suspect.

The public was also trying to help out in any way that they could. By Wednesday, July 12, the police had received more than 100 tips from the public, and that number continued to grow every day. The press reported that there had already been one sighting of Dagenais, which the RCMP was quickly trying to follow up. On Saturday, two separate groups of people reported seeing a man matching Curtis Dagenais' description standing in a ditch along Highway 12, between the intersection of Highway 12, Highway 3 and Martin's Lake Regional Park, at about 12:45 PM. Of concern was that the individual was spotted approximately 32 kilometres from the site of the gun battle, well outside the search boundary established by the police team.

By Sunday, however, the sighting was discarded. Investigators stated they had consulted with individuals who knew Dagenais and who also saw the man matching his description on Saturday. Those people said they didn't think the person they saw was Curtis Dagenais, and the investigators agreed. One possible lead had now evaporated into none.

There was little change in Cameron's and Bourdages' condition as the week went on—still listed as critical. The RCMP finally issued a Canada-wide warrant for the arrest of Curtis Dagenais, yet only one charge appeared on the warrant. The authorities decided to lay a charge of attempted murder— concerning the gun battle between Dagenais and Constable Knopp. An investigator told the media that all they needed was one charge to issue the nationwide warrant, and he refused to comment when asked if the nature of the warrant had anything to do with the fact that Cameron's and Bourdages' medical condition had not stabilized.

On Tuesday, July 11, Arthur Dagenais finally appeared in court in North Battleford on the two charges facing him, then returned Wednesday morning for a bail hearing. The Crown prosecutor on the case made it known that he vehemently opposed any release for the elder Dagenais.

Documents filed with the court indicated that Arthur had been arrested trying to re-enter a crime scene after being told not to. The crime scene in question was his farm, and a staff sergeant supervising the property in the early morning hours of Saturday, July 8, had told two constables to follow Arthur. When the elderly man drove towards his farm, the officers trailing him placed him under arrest.

Further information revealed at the hearing indicated the police had conducted a thorough search of the farmhouse and land. They'd found two rifles and $27,000 in cash stuffed in two toolboxes in one of the combines on the farm. One resident later commented that Arthur didn't believe in banks.

But a search of the home turned up more firearms, including an unregistered .22-calibre rifle, hence the second charge.

Other testimony at the hearing revealed more of what occurred the night of the shooting. The Crown alleged that Curtis called the RCMP to ask for their assistance in removing his sister Grace from the house he owned with his mother, a request the RCMP declined. Curtis decided to handle the matter himself. Fearing what might happen, Arthur phoned a provincial number for the RCMP telling them what was taking place, but again there was no response from the police. The Crown alleged that later that evening, Curtis called Arthur from his cell phone and told him he was fleeing from the police. Curtis was apparently crying because he wasn't sure his old truck could hold up for much longer.

The Crown also tendered statements from Arthur during the hearing, in which he apparently blamed the police for the situation because they "forced his son into a corner." Arthur also told police they would have something to worry about if anything happened to his son.

The statements were all that was needed for the provincial court judge who heard the case to make her decision. Citing Arthur's longtime animosity towards police, Judge Violet Meekma returned to court on Friday, July 15, stating that Arthur would be a risk to the safety of the public and police officers if he was released, and would also likely try to re-enter the crime scene. Meekma subsequently ordered Arthur held without bail and scheduled him to enter a plea on July 26.

By the time Arthur's case had been heard, more information about the condition of Cameron and Bourdages had leaked to the media, and none of it was good. An anonymous source reported that both officers had been shot in the head, and that Cameron, considered to be in the worst condition, was on life support.

"It's not looking good for them. There's a lot of prayers for them right now," the source said. Another report confirmed that the police cruiser in which the two had been travelling had three bullet holes through the windshield.

Yet finding the suspect who was responsible for the shootings was proving to be more difficult than anyone had imagined. By Thursday, July 13, the RCMP scaled back their search. Officers from other detachments and provinces were sent home. Checkpoints were moved closer to the crime scene, while a 24-hour police presence patrolled the streets and surrounding area of Spiritwood. In total, the RCMP had searched between 30 and 40 buildings, abandoned farmhouses, granaries, huts, sheds and shacks inside the target area.

"We've satisfied ourselves to the extent possible that the suspect is not in that area," RCMP Superintendent Rob Nason stated.

The tips kept pouring in, mostly about hitchhikers and suggestions of places the RCMP should try looking. There were 140 tips logged by Thursday afternoon. The police also hosted a community meeting, which 150 people attended, concerning the events of the last week. The public was frightened that an alleged killer was still on the loose, and the police were no closer to finding him.

On Sunday, July 16, that fear was paired with sadness when it was announced that Constables Robin Cameron and Marc Bourdages had died. Cameron died first at 11:00 PM on Saturday night when her family made the heart-wrenching decision to take her off life support. Two hours later, as if he didn't want to see his partner patrol the hereafter without backup, Bourdages succumbed to his wounds at 1:15 AM.

The Canada-wide warrant for Curtis Dagenais was promptly updated from one count of attempted murder to include two counts of first-degree murder.

∽

Flags flew at half-mast as the community, the RCMP and the nation as a whole mourned the deaths of two of their own.

In a stoic display of bravery, Bourdages' widow Natasha issued a statement shortly after her husband died.

"I believe that Marc is with us now in spirit and that he is in a better place where he can be peaceful," she said.

More information continued to come to light as the scaled-back search for Curtis Dagenais continued. A report surfaced that Arthur had sought a private prosecution in 1993 against some police officers, claiming they had beat him up. The charge had been stayed by the Crown.

Court documents also revealed just whose side Arthur was on. Apparently, Arthur had driven to Elsie's home after the shooting to confront his daughter.

"I hope you're happy now. Two policemen were shot," he allegedly told Grace.

The *Globe and Mail* published an article on July 18, stating that it took more than an hour for the Mounties to call in an ambulance. The shooting had occurred at approximately 9:15 PM, but the local ambulance crew stated they didn't get a call to respond until 10:24 PM. The RCMP had no comment.

In the meantime, funeral plans were announced for the two officers. Beardy's Okemasis First Nation would hold a three-day wake for Robin Cameron starting July 19, culminating in a regimental funeral on July 21. Marc Bourdages' regimental funeral would take place at the Depot chapel in Regina on July 25, followed by a private family internment.

The deaths of the two officers seemed to bring about a lull in the search. But events quickly heated up once the weekend ended. On Tuesday, July 18, the RCMP received word that the *Edmonton Sun*, a tabloid daily newspaper in Alberta's capital city, had received a five-page letter, allegedly signed by Curtis Dagenais. The police quickly obtained a warrant for the letter, which they discovered had been posted on July 14 in Shell Lake, 30 kilometres away from the crime scene and outside the search area.

"I feel terrible about what has happened, but they would not leave me alone," stated the letter, which was published in both the *Edmonton* and *Calgary Sun*.

"When I backed away with my pick-up, I didn't realize my steering was turned the wrong way and crowded Grace a bit but was not intentional. But Elsie and Grace can wrap any RCMP around their little finger."

The letter went on, detailing the confrontation with the police, the chase and blaming Dagenais' sister for much of what had happened.

"Cameron said I was under arrest for assault and assault with a weapon. I couldn't believe it. I had a screaming match with my sister, but never touched her."

During the chase, the police "would ram me hard, hoping to spin me out of control, hoping that I would roll."

The letter writer also claimed the officers started shooting first, before he'd even exited the truck.

"They wanted to kill me, to hush me about their dirty work," stated the letter.

As for Grace, he claimed he and his mother owned the property, "not my sister, who I wanted removed...because she has told me things to mislead me, to give herself more time to screw me over as to division of family property due to the divorce."

The letter writer also stated that he took off because he felt fleeing the police "was within my rights."

The RCMP successfully obtained the letter from the *Sun,* which was handed over for experts to examine. They wanted to compare the handwriting in the letter to samples of Dagenais' handwriting to prove he was the one who penned it. Family members reported they were confident he had written the letter. Elsie promptly issued a public plea for Curtis to turn himself in.

Meanwhile, the people of Shell Lake were shocked to discover the letter had been mailed from their small resort town. One resident stated other homeowners were deliberately leaving their keys inside their vehicles so that, if Dagenais came around, he wouldn't break into their homes looking for a ride.

Arthur made another appearance in court on July 18, moving the date up one week at his own request so he could enter a not guilty plea. The judge, however, informed him he couldn't enter a plea until after his preliminary hearing, which was scheduled for December 5. The preliminary hearing would only deal with the obstruction charge—thanks to a one-year amnesty for gun owners with unregistered firearms announced by the Conservative government of Prime Minister Stephen Harper, the Crown was forced to stay the weapons charge.

And then something happened. At approximately 4:00 PM that same day, after an 11-day manhunt that had consumed countless police hours and resources, a farming couple from Mildred pulled up in front of the Spiritwood RCMP detachment. Curtis Dagenais exited their vehicle, walked into the detachment and turned himself in without a fight.

~

For a man who had spent 11 days and nights in the bush, Curtis was in good condition when he surrendered to police, but the reason for that quickly became obvious. Besides an ankle injury that left him limping, Dagenais was fine. As a precaution, the police transported him under heavy escort to hospital, where he was given a clean bill of health. He was then lodged in cells until his first court appearance.

The arrest was made public at a hastily arranged press conference at Depot, after both the Cameron and Bourdages families had been informed of Dagenais' surrender.

"The first priority was to notify the families of Robin Cameron and Marc Bourdages," Assistant Commissioner Darrell McFayden stated.

Other police officers described the mood within the ranks after the surrender as "absolute relief from top to bottom." The couple who drove Curtis to Spiritwood were also the people who had found him. Armand and Rosanne Smith were out haying Tuesday afternoon when they found Curtis in their field.

"We were supposed to be haying all day. That didn't happen," Rosanne told reporters.

Initially, Rosanne and Armand said little to the press, only that upon finding him, they had talked to him a lot before convincing him to turn himself in.

"We just talked and he decided to give himself up and thank God he did," Rosanne said. "The only thing we told him was that it would be better for him to do this than to, you know, commit hara-kiri or something. We just kept telling him it was the best thing to do."

Rosanna refused to go into detail. When asked if Dagenais was a family friend, Rosanne only replied "We've known him."

A friend of the Smiths who listened to the story over coffee with the family later filled in some of the gaps for the press. Dagenais had allegedly told the couple he was only in the target search area shortly after the shooting, at which time he quickly made his way to Arthur's home to change his clothes and grab supplies. He skipped north of the search area by the second day, moving constantly, but was never more than a few miles away. He slept in grain bins, tractors and the bush, breaking into farmhouses when there was no one home and stealing small bits of food. He denied that anyone had helped him during his escape.

The source also told the press the conversation between Dagenais and the Smiths lasted six hours—three hours out in the field, then another three hours over coffee at the Smiths' home. Curtis talked about killing himself, but Rosanne talked him out of that. Instead, she convinced the 41-year-old to turn himself in.

~

Curtis Dagenais limped into court for his first appearance on Wednesday, July 19, wearing a dark T-shirt and pants. He stood in the prisoner box with his arms crossed and muttered what would be the first of many confusing statements throughout the court process. After the clerk of the court read all three charges to him, she asked Dagenais if he understood the charges.

"No," he replied.

The charges were promptly read again. This time Curtis replied in the affirmative.

Dagenais' arrest wasn't the only news making the rounds. The RCMP issued a statement clarifying an earlier *Globe and Mail* report about the time it took for the ambulance to arrive on scene. The original incident, they stated, took place at 9:15 PM. The chase ended at 10:15, and the ambulance was called at approximately 10:25.

The *Globe and Mail* responded with another article, this one stating that the police cruiser had collided with the vehicle it was chasing, causing the airbags to deploy, which would have left Cameron and Bourdages helpless. Yet photos of the cruiser showed no visible front-end damage. There was also no word on the location of the murder weapon.

While the Crown started to build its case against Curtis Dagenais, the RCMP turned its attention to burying its dead. Starting on Thursday, approximately 200 people attended Cameron's three-day wake on her home reserve. Five officers dressed in red serge presented her daughter Shayne and Cameron's parents with a black, red, yellow and white star blanket, emblazoned with the RCMP crest. The casket was put on display at the local hockey arena, draped in the Canadian flag, with Cameron's Stetson placed at the top. A table was set up so that mourners could drop off cards, pictures and flowers, as well as cigarettes, which symbolized the Native tradition of giving tobacco. Books of condolence were also sent to every RCMP detachment across the country so that the public could share their thoughts and feelings.

"She left us way too soon," Milton Gamble, one of Cameron's relatives said. "It's always hard to lose a young person; it's even harder when you lose a family member who carried so much weight in the community as a role model."

Later, at Cameron's regimental funeral, one of her sisters read out a letter to the thousands of peace officers from across North America who attended, written by Cameron's daughter Shayne as Robin lay dying.

"I love you so much. You are my world. I'm telling you this with my tears and prayers, I will see you again someday... you're not going away forever."

Bourdages' funeral was just as emotional. The service was held in the same small chapel on the Depot grounds where he and Natasha had wed only a few years earlier, with the same celebrant who married them now guiding a mass of over 1000 officers in mourning his loss. Again Natasha set aside her own grief to offer her thoughts and words to the assembled audience.

"Our happily-ever-after has now been interrupted. I know he left this Earth knowing that he was loved, and I know he loved us. I know Marc is in a better place now where there is no evil or pain, where there is no sickness or sorrow, and for that I'm glad."

RCMP Commissioner Zaccardelli also attended the funeral, sharing some words with the audience, but speaking directly to Natasha.

"I don't know if it makes it harder or easier for you that you, too, are a Mountie," the commissioner said, reminding Natasha that the "family" of the RCMP would be there for her. All the while Luca, dressed in a tiny red serge, watched.

~

While the funerals made headlines, there was more news still to come as both Arthur and Curtis prepared for their days in court.

A search of records revealed an outstanding lawsuit Arthur had filed against three police officers in March 2005. According to the complaint, Elsie had filed a private prosecution against Arthur in January 2004, which had been stayed by the Crown. In the $1 million suit, Arthur accused the three officers of malicious prosecution—in essence that the officers pursued the case even though they knew the allegation was unfounded. He also claimed he had not received full disclosure of the evidence against him, that his Charter rights had been violated and that as a result of the accusation, he suffered from emotional stress, anxiety, depression, humiliation, loss of reputation, self-esteem and income, as well as psychiatric illness.

Unfortunately for Arthur, he had missed an important deadline in the suit for serving statements of claim on the defendants.

In August, Arthur decided to apply for a bail review with the help of attorney Lori Gollan in the Court of Queen's Bench. The Crown argued that Arthur posed a risk to the public and police, and that he had been abusive in the past to both his wife and children. The Crown suggested Arthur might know the location of the murder weapon and pointed out that several Spiritwood residents had signed a petition demanding Arthur not be allowed to return to the community.

Gollan argued that her client had been in jail long enough already to have served any sentence he might have received on the obstruction of justice charge.

"Art may be an angry man....In Canada, we don't incarcerate people for being angry," she said.

During the review, Arthur admitted that Curtis had called him during the chase and wanted his father to meet him at a certain spot so that Arthur could be a witness when the police arrested him. However, Arthur took the wrong road and got lost.

Gollan closed her arguments by asking for no bail conditions for her client, but said Arthur had agreed to wear an electronic monitoring device if granted bail. Justice Donald Krueger announced he would deliver his verdict on August 14.

On Thursday, August 3, the community of Spiritwood hosted a community remembrance and healing service. Two Mounties in red serge marched in wearing Cameron's and Bourdages' Stetsons. Natasha, Luca and Shayne attended the ceremony, as did Elsie and Grace Dagenais.

"We have to heal the same as the community. This started off as a family tragedy, and it ended up being a community tragedy. My mom is part of the community. I'm a part of the community," Grace said.

On August 14, Krueger ruled that Arthur would be released from custody, pending the posting of a $1500 cash bond.

Although he was not required to wear a monitoring device, Krueger ordered Arthur to stay on his ranch and not go into the community of Spiritwood.

"All Arthur Dagenais wishes to do is go home, where he has lived all his life, and attend to his business," Krueger stated, who attached several other conditions to the release, including a list of 20 people consisting mostly of family members, witnesses for his son's case and certain RCMP officers, active and retired, who Arthur was forbidden from communicating with. He was also to report to Shellbrook RCMP and a bail supervisor twice per week and abstain from having any firearms in his possession or consuming alcohol. He was to travel no farther than six kilometres from his ranch house at any given time.

Curtis' case was also beginning. In an appearance on August 17, the court asked Curtis to verbally agree to a disclosure of evidence agreement with the Crown in which Curtis was not allowed to discuss the evidence against him with anyone, including his father. The only exception was a statement Arthur made to the police. Curtis agreed.

Because she was representing both father and son in related cases, many, including Crown prosecutor Scott Bartlett, started to wonder out loud if Gollan might be facing a conflict of interest. Gollan denied the claim, but on November 2, 2006, she withdrew as counsel for both Arthur and Curtis, citing differences of opinion, as well as the strain on her practice.

Curtis was being kept in secure custody at the Saskatoon Correctional Centre, where he was only allowed out of his cell for 15 minutes per day provided no more than two other inmates were out as well. He was visibly alarmed by Gollan's move.

"I'm more concerned about some information and evidence Ms. Gollan has in her possession, the security of that. I'm worried about it being destroyed or getting into the wrong hands and being destroyed," Curtis told the court. Gollan responded that she was obligated to return all of the disclosure to the Crown as well as return to Curtis any materials he had given her.

On December 14, Curtis forced another delay when he informed the court that his new lawyer had withdrawn from the case and that his application for legal aid had been denied. He asked the court to appoint him an attorney because he could not afford one of his own. Curtis also stated he wanted counsel from "outside the province as this court is involved."

Bartlett informed the court that he had sent a police officer to Saskatoon to see if Curtis had a lawyer, but the defendant had refused to see the officer.

"He was sending them to the correctional centre to harass me. He had no business being there," Curtis replied.

Judge Violet Meekma adjourned the hearing so that Bartlett could phone legal aid to verify Curtis' application had been denied. Bartlett returned to court and said the department wouldn't release the information without Curtis' consent, which he refused to give.

"I want to seek advice about the private information on that letter being possession of the Crown," Dagenais stated, which put him and the court in a Catch 22—Dagenais wanted a lawyer to prove he didn't qualify for legal aid, but in order to do that, Dagenais needed to hire a lawyer, which he couldn't afford. Meekma adjourned the hearing for one week so that Dagenais could get advice, but not before Curtis offered up a theory of his own. "Election time. That's what they're trying to avoid," he said.

When court reconvened on December 21, Curtis promptly asked for another week to seek advice. Meekma refused, stating that the March 5 preliminary hearing was approaching, and they risked losing the court time.

"Is that a threat? That sounds like a threat," Dagenais responded.

Meekma instead questioned Dagenais under oath about his financial assets. Convinced he couldn't afford a lawyer of his own, she appointed counsel for him. High-profile Saskatoon lawyer Bill Roe expressed an interest in taking the case, but he wasn't available for the dates set and also had to arrange a fee schedule with the province.

By the time both issues were sorted out, the preliminary inquiry had been delayed to August 13, 2007, with Roe as the defence lawyer.

On January 27, 2007, with his own court date looming, an interview with Arthur Dagenais was published in several papers in which he defended his son and blamed the police.

"They wanted him dead, there's no doubt about it," Arthur said. "He's not a cop killer."

Arthur also showed the reporter a copy of a letter sent from the department of justice stating his phone line had been tapped. When asked if he knew where the murder weapon was, Arthur suddenly became less talkative.

"I'm not saying anything," he replied.

Arthur's trial lasted one day. On May 18, 2007, the older Dagenais was acquitted of the charge against him. The judge ruled that, because the two constables following Arthur had arrested him before he reached the crime scene, there was no way to tell which way he was definitely headed. By August 2007, Arthur was asking the provincial government for compensation for wrongful arrest.

On August 13, Curtis Dagenais entered a courtroom to begin his preliminary hearing, shoeless, dressed in a purple long-sleeve T-shirt and black pants. Judge Earl Kalenith immediately ordered a publication ban surrounding the evidence the court was to hear, which included 2400 pages of disclosure and approximately 33 witnesses.

On August 21, the hearing was forced to continue without Dagenais when he became ill while listening to the testimony of a forensic pathologist. Curtis turned pale, nearly fainting from the graphic testimony, and was taken away to lie down. He was returned to the courtroom when the witness completed his testimony.

"Mr. Dagenais has a phobia about blood," Roe told reporters.

One day later, Kalenith deemed there was sufficient evidence for Curtis to stand trial on all charges.

Before long Arthur was back in the news, calling for the return of the guns and $27,000 seized in what he claimed was an illegal search of his home. It was a strange situation because the Crown had applied for the guns to be destroyed, even though Arthur had been found not guilty. He was given a list of 36 items seized from his home, almost all of which had been blacked out except the money and guns. When she learned of the money, Elsie asked the court to hold the money, which she claimed Arthur was hiding because of their divorce proceedings.

On January 10, 2008, it was announced that Curtis Dagenais would stand trial by jury in North Battleford from September 15 to October 10, 2008. He is presently being held in custody without bail.

Chapter Four

Detective Daniel Tessier

Killed: *March 2, 2007, Laval, Québec*
Accused: *Basil Parasiris*
Charges: *First-degree murder; attempted murder;*
attempt to wound by discharging a firearm;
endangering life by discharging a firearm
Status: *Acquitted on all counts*

~

Friday, June 13, 2008

There is no experience quite as nerve-racking as waiting for a jury to make its decision. Once the judge instructs the 12-person jury, it is sequestered to deliberate the fate of the accused, and the world outside the courtroom seems to grind to a halt. The Crown and defence lawyers are issued pagers that beep when the jury is returning to the courtroom, sometimes with a verdict, sometimes to ask for more clarification of their instructions and the law upholding them, or to rehear taped evidence or transcribed statements.

The judge overseeing the trial seldom leaves the court-house until the jury has either come to a verdict or concluded their deliberations for the day. Members of the media sign in with the clerk of the court to be notified by phone or pager of the jury's return. Some go back to their offices, while others pull out books or laptops and set up shop outside the courtroom, waiting. Sometimes they even play cards.

Members of the accused's and victim's families roam the halls of the courthouse or find comfortable seats and wait, tapping toes against the floor as the minutes drag past agonizingly. If the accused is free on bail, he or she might join family and friends. Otherwise the accused is confined to a holding cell within the courthouse.

The victim of the crime might also wait around to learn the fate of the accused. In this case, however, the victim wasn't present. Detective Sergeant Daniel Tessier was dead and had been for well over a year, shot to death by a man during a raid on his home. The trial of the man accused of Tessier's murder had wound on for more than four gruelling weeks. Four days earlier, the jury had received its instructions from the judge and gone into seclusion. They emerged only once to ask to listen to some of the evidence presented at trial. But not a peep had been heard from them since.

Late in the afternoon of June 13, 2008, a frenzy broke out, sparked by a series of cell phone calls and pager beeps. The Crown and defence lawyers rushed back into the Superior Courthouse in Longueuil, Québec, followed by members of the media and the family of the victim and the accused. The clerk of the court unlocked the courtroom and confirmed to all that the jury had reached a verdict.

The justice of the court took his place, and the jury members filed into their seats. The accused, a Brossard resident by the name of Basil Parasiris, tried to remain calm as he stood at the justice's request. The room was virtually silent. Parasiris' wife shook in her seat, wringing her hands while at the other side of the room, members of the Service de police de la ville de Laval held their breath.

Tessier's widow, also a police officer, was nowhere to be seen.

At the judge's request, the foreman of the jury stood and affirmed that the group had reached a verdict. With every ear hanging on the words that would emerge from the foreman's lips, the juror opened his mouth to speak, and almost moving as one, everyone in the courtroom leaned forward to listen.

In the early morning hours of March 2, 2007, the sun hadn't yet begun to crest the eastern horizon, which was good news for all the police officers gathered around the well-appointed home in Brossard. There was no movement from inside the home, which made them even happier. The more quickly they could enter the home to execute their warrant using the element of surprise, the sooner the risk of the operation would be behind them.

They weren't the only officers from the Laval Police Department out on the streets that morning. Across the city of Laval, groups of officers were preparing to raid seven other properties—six in Laval itself and one other in Brossard. The focus of the raids was the ever-present leech on the back of civilized society—drugs.

The officers at the home in Brossard, on Rimouski Crescent, however, took little for granted. Based on the evidence collected to date, they believed the home they were preparing to search was more significant than the others. Inside, they deduced, lived one of the kingpins of a crack-cocaine drug ring that operated in Laval.

The operation had been long and extensive. In 2006, Constable François Leblanc, a detective with the Laval drug and morality squad, had received a tip from his policing counterparts in Montréal that three people were selling cocaine out of a local bar in Laval, called Bar le Skratch.

Few details were associated with the tip, other than that one of the dealers was known as "Mani." As the investigation progressed, officers were able to identify "Mani" as one Emmanuel Maroudis, and they had linked him to at least four other dealers in the area.

One month after receiving the original tip, Leblanc authorized an undercover officer to make a buy. The officer went to Bar le Skratch and purchased half a gram of cocaine from a dealer, who turned out to be Maroudis himself. The buys continued, and by October 25, 2006, officers had made several undercover purchases of cocaine. At that point, Leblanc authorized his team to ask for larger amounts, hoping the demand would reveal an important detail in the drug ring—the location of the "stash." In police lingo, the stash is the location where drug dealers keep the bulk of their product. Once they found the stash, the squad figured they could bust the ring and remove it from the streets permanently.

Just weeks after officers started asking for larger quantities of cocaine during undercover buys, the case took a twist. A patrol officer pulled over one of the other drug dealers for speeding—a young man named Nikolaos Xanthis, who was associated with Maroudis. At the time, Xanthis was driving a green Pontiac Grand Prix. The car, however, was not registered to him—the registration came back to a man named Basil Parasiris, who lived in nearby Brossard. The police ran a check on Parasiris' name, but the result came back clean—no criminal record to speak of, and though his name wasn't forgotten, he wasn't thought to be in anyway associated with the drug ring. That began to change, however, as the squad continued to watch both Xanthis and Maroudis.

One week after stopping Xanthis—but not arresting him—the team started a surveillance operation focused on Xanthis. One night, the team tailing him watched as he entered a duplex in Brossard. Further surveillance of the duplex revealed that no one seemed to actually live there. The Laval drug squad became increasingly confident that they had finally located the stash.

One night, the surveillance team watched as Xanthis drove to a nearby business, went into a back office and started selling drugs inside. The business in question was actually a pair of establishments—one was called Golf-O-Max, an indoor virtual driving range for golfers. The second business adjoining Golf-O-Max was a bar. Both establishments, according to corporate records, were part owned by Basil Parasiris. Suddenly, Parasiris was back on the squad's radar.

Later that night, Xanthis returned to the duplex that the police were watching then drove to a nearby home listed as owned by Basil Parasiris. Xanthis stayed in the house for approximately 30 minutes, then returned to the duplex.

On February 27, 2007, the surveillance squad watched as a vehicle registered to Parasiris' wife (Penny Gounis) stopped outside the duplex. Although Parasiris was never positively identified by any of the officers watching, the squad thought they saw Parasiris enter the duplex, then leave. Unfortunately, the identity of the man was never confirmed.

Xanthis wasn't the only person police were watching. They attached a surveillance beacon to Maroudis' car. An analysis of his travel patterns showed that between December 2006 and February 1, 2007, Maroudis had been near Parasiris' home at least 10 times. He was also at the Golf-O-Max twice during that time period.

On the same day that the travel analysis was carried out, the Montréal police contacted the Laval Police Department.

They had received another tip from an informant who stated that the owner of a business called the Golf-O-Max was linked to cocaine trafficking in the area. Laval police, confident that they knew who the dealers were and that the stash location was at the duplex in Brossard, prepared a series of search and arrest warrants for a large scale, same-day operation to bust the trafficking ring. Based on the tip, police decided to include Parasiris' house in the raid. The circumstantial evidence seemed enough to tie him to the ring, if not pinpoint him as the kingpin in the trafficking operation. In the affidavit filed with the justice of the peace in requesting the search warrants, the police argued they still had enough cause to justify a search of the home. The justice of the peace granted the warrant, as well as several others.

The bulk of the warrants were relatively straightforward and were all drafted to be executed on the same day—March 2, 2007. Of the eight warrants requested, six were simple "knock and search" warrants, in which the police physically knock on the door of a home during daylight hours and show the owner a copy of the warrant. Initially, Laval police were planning to ask for a similar warrant for Parasiris' home. But the more they thought about it, the more they wondered if Parasiris' theoretical status within the drug ring might require a different approach.

Parasiris' house was one of two homes selected for a so-called dynamic entry, or no-knock, warrant. The warrant meant the police could raid the home at night, and they didn't have to knock. They were still going to, but with a much larger device than a fist—the officers conducting the raid had a battering ram ready to knock down the front door. Once the door was down, the raid team would storm the home as quickly as possible, securing all of the individuals inside before conducting their search. No-knock warrants are typically served by Special Weapons And Tactics (SWAT) teams or RCMP Emergency Response Teams (ERT), given the risky nature of the raid. The Laval police department, however, was trained in dynamic entry warrants and was confident they could carry the raid out on their own.

The second dynamic entry warrant for a raid on the stash duplex was a no-brainer. If the police knocked first and waited, whoever was inside could destroy the evidence police needed by doing something as simple as flushing the toilet. While police planned their early-morning raid for the stash house, the team broached a hypothetical—what if word of the raid reached Parasiris before they could execute their warrant? That might give him, if he was as high up on the totem pole as they suspected, time to destroy evidence and even flee the scene. The police asked for and received a dynamic entry warrant for Parasiris' home in Brossard as well.

At 5:00 AM on March 2, the officers participating in the raid were making final preparations. Some adjusted their bullet-proof vests, emblazoned with the word "POLICE" on the front and back. Others made sure their ball caps fit just right, and everyone double-checked their weapons to make sure, in the worst-case scenario, they were ready for battle.

～

In a way, the morning raid represented a rebirth for Detective Daniel Tessier. The 42-year-old Québecer was a 17-year veteran of the Laval Police Department but had only been attached to the drug and morality squad for little over a week. It wasn't really anything new for Tessier—in his long career with Laval, it was his second stint with the squad.

Tessier had spent his entire life in "la belle province." He was originally from Bonsecours in the Eastern Townships region and studied at the Collège d'enseignement général et professionel (CEGEP) de Sherbrooke. He gave up his studies in civil engineering to become a police officer in Laval, where he spent the first 10 years in patrol before moving on to a temporary stint in the drug and morality department. Shortly afterwards, Tessier transferred to a special investigations unit, then made the jump back to the drug squad. After some specialized training, including how to properly conduct a dynamic entry, Tessier returned to the squad and was now ready to participate in the morning's activities. As a veteran, Tessier was already well schooled in the ways of dynamic entries. In a sense, these types of raids were old hat—he had taken part in numerous raids over the course of his career.

"He wanted to return to the drug squad because he wanted to finish the work he started," said Nathalie Laurin, a spokesperson for the police department.

Outside of his police duties, Tessier also ran a successful home security business. And, as is the case with many police officers, he'd married a police officer. His wife, Dominique Lapointe, was a serving officer in Repentigny. The couple had two daughters—Marie-Andrée, 13 years old, and Veronique, who was 12.

Tessier liked to keep busy. He had just finished building a home in the Eastern Townships and also shared a waterfront home in Repentigny with Dominique. He was a happy, friendly individual devoted to the police force.

"He was always in a good mood. He had a beautiful smile and was always the one to cheer up his fellow officers when they had tough times," said Reverend Raymond Gravel, a former chaplain for the Laval Police Department.

⁓

The Laval police team prepared in advance for the March 2 raid on the house in Brossard. They studied the layout of the house, as well as watched the family so that they could plan their entry properly. Each officer was assigned a specific quadrant in the raid.

Tessier and Constable Serge Lauzon, the first officers through the door, were responsible for securing the master bedroom on the second floor, on top of a winding staircase. Other officers were assigned to the rooms of the two children believed to be inside—a 15-year-old boy and a seven-year-old girl. Constable Stéphane Forbes, 46, was tapped to secure the young girl's bedroom.

Each member suited up in bulletproof vests and checked their 9 mm sidearms, holding them at the ready. There were only four people inside the home—two adults and two children—and the darkness inside suggested that they were all asleep.

Shortly after 5:00 AM, Constable François Leblanc gave the okay to the rest of the squad to begin the raid. They lined up outside the front door of the Brossard home, battering ram in tow. On command, all those clutching the ram began pounding it against the door. It took three solid bangs before the door finally fell from its hinges, exposing the interior. The team sprinted inside, all of them shouting the worlds "Police!" at the top of their lungs. The second officer through the door was Daniel Tessier.

The interior of the home was dark. The only light came from outside, courtesy of a skylight at the top of the winding staircase. The entire team bolted up the staircase, orienting themselves within the home so that they knew exactly where they were supposed to go. Within seconds, Lauzon reached the top of the staircase.

Then all hell broke loose.

~

Lauzon reached the second floor, with Tessier right behind him. Their target—the master bedroom—was to their left.

But instead of turning left, Lauzon turned right, leaving Tessier alone in front of the master bedroom. Lauzon rushed up to the door in front of him, turned the doorknob and pushed. Instead of opening completely, the door slid open only a few millimetres, then stopped. Lauzon could feel resistance coming from the other side of the door. He kept pushing.

∽

Meanwhile, Forbes, who was assigned the task of securing the bedroom at the top of the stairs, directly ahead of the team, rushed to his target. The room, the squad believed, belonged to seven-year-old Stephanie Parasiris. Forbes reached down for the doorknob, turned it and opened the door, sticking his head inside.

∽

Tessier was now left alone in front of the master bedroom. He was approaching the door when it suddenly flew open. In the shadows stood a figure. There was no time to think or react. The darkness was suddenly illuminated by flash, and the roar of a high-powered gun cut through the house like a scythe. Three more flashes and blasts echoed through the upstairs. Daniel Tessier fell to the ground like a stone.

∽

Forbes was just entering the bedroom of Stephanie Parasiris when he heard gunshots. Before he could react, he felt something smack into his right arm, which instantly went limp.
Reacting on instinct, Forbes continued into the bedroom. Unable
to holster his gun, he ditched it behind a TV set in the bedroom.
Stephanie was sitting on her bed, crying for her mother. Forbes
could feel warm blood gushing from his arm, but he tried to
reassure the girl, telling her he was a police officer.

⁓

Lauzon was still struggling with the blocked door when
the sounds of gunfire erupted. The reverberations of the shots
and prompt return fire made for a confusing sound environ-
ment, so much so that Lauzon thought the shots were being
fired from behind the door he was trying to open, when in fact
the gunfire was coming from behind him. Lauzon raised his
gun and started firing into the blocked door in front of him,
retreating backwards as he did so.

The bedroom he was trying to access belonged to the
Parasiris' 15-year-old son George.

⁓

Sergeant Nathalie Allard had just reached the top of the
stairs when the flash and roar of gunfire echoed over the cacoph-
ony of sound on the second level. She heard the direction the
gunfire was coming from, saw Tessier crumple to the ground
and immediately took aim and opened fire on the master bedroom, as did several other officers around her.

Allard had just fired off several rounds when she felt someone collide into her as she pulled the trigger for another shot. The impact of the collision knocked her off her feet, which also changed the trajectory of her aim. Her 9 mm barked, followed seconds later by a sudden cry of pain from inside the master bedroom.

Allard turned. The man who had run into her was Lauzon. Amid the gunfire, the pair quickly retreated into the nearby bathroom. Allard glanced down and saw blood on her hands. Lauzon looked her over but couldn't find any bullet wounds.

~

Stephanie Parasiris wasn't getting any calmer, and Constable Stéphane Forbes wasn't feeling any better. Blood continued to seep from the bullet wound in his arm. He could tell from both the size of the wound and the impact with which it had struck that the round likely came from a large calibre weapon, larger than his sidearm at least.

The room was starting to spin, and Forbes could feel himself growing increasingly disoriented and tired. Knowing he was losing a lot of blood and afraid of passing out in Stephanie's bedroom, the 17-year police veteran told the girl to stay inside, then turned around and walked out the door and down the stairs, collapsing into the arms of two other officers.

~

Inside his bedroom, George had no idea what was going on. He'd heard a crash, heard the sound of feet running up the stairs and then heard gunfire, some of which seemed to be coming from right outside the second door to his room, the door he had put his computer desk against. The 15-year-old alertly reached for the telephone in his room and dialed 911.

∽

The gunfire was starting to die down, consisting mostly of the pops of 9 mm police-issue sidearms. Inside the upstairs bathroom, Lauzon was feeling afraid and frustrated. Having checked out Allard and finding no apparent injury, he instructed her to call 911 for an ambulance. Lauzon looked out into the hallway. He could see Tessier, collapsed on the floor in front of the master bedroom.

He also saw the door to Stephanie Parasiris' bedroom slowly open, and the seven-year-old girl wandered out into the hallway. Poised at the bathroom door, Lauzon and Allard both started beckoning frantically at the child to come to them, to get her out of harm's way. The girl complied, collapsing into Allard's arms. With Stephanie safe, Lauzon darted out of her bedroom and grabbed Tessier, dragging him into her room.

Trying to contain his anger, Lauzon shouted towards the master bedroom, his heavily accented English booming so loudly it was recorded by the 911 dispatcher who had answered Allard's call.

"You will show me your hands from behind the door. This is the police here. You have shot a police officer."

At first there was no response from the master bedroom. Then the voice of a woman shouting "Oh my God!" reached Lauzon's ears and also the radio Allard was using. A man slowly emerged from the bedroom, crawling on his hands and knees. Within a heartbeat the police converged on him, cuffing his hands behind his back and dragging him down the stairs, just as the first ambulance arrived on scene.

Lauzon personally handed Basil Parasiris off to two other officers and was about to turn away, but he could not swallow the rage that had built up inside him. He whirled around, grabbed Parasiris by the neck and drew back his fist as if preparing to punch him in the face. Instead, Lauzon dropped his hand and spoke,

"Mon hostie de sale," he muttered coldly, French for "You f****** asshole."

∾

Inside his bedroom, George was speaking with the 911 operator.

"Yeah, there are guys shooting in my house...I don't know what's happening."

The 911 operator asked George if he could look out his window. When he complied, she asked if he could see any police cars. George confirmed he could see two.

∾

Two ambulances arrived on scene within minutes of one another. The first crew rushed inside, scooped up Daniel Tessier and raced out of the house as one officer performed CPR. The stretcher was rolled into the back of the ambulance, which took off, lights and sirens blazing, for Charles LeMoyne Hospital in Greenfield Park.

Forbes was loaded into the second ambulance and promptly taken away.

Approximately half an hour later, a third ambulance, followed shortly thereafter by a fourth, arrived at the Parasiris' house.

~

Inside the master bedroom, Penny Gounis, Parasiris' wife, was pressing a towel against her arm, trying to stop the bleeding. She had been trying to hide inside the bedroom's walk-in closet during the gun battle when a bullet, appearing as if from nowhere, struck her arm.

An officer approached her and informed her she was under arrest. Gounis was forced to drop the towel as the officer handcuffed her hands behind her back, led her into the upstairs hallway and sat her down on the floor, then left.

Penny looked around and spotted Stephanie, still cowering in the bathroom. Gounis slid her way across the floor towards the bathroom to console her daughter but could not ignore the pain in her arm, nor the blood gushing from it.

Lauzon passed by. Penny finally spoke up.

"Could you please call an ambulance before I die?" she asked him. The cop acquiesced, though acted coldly, Penny thought.

After what felt like an eternity, a paramedic arrived on scene. By this point Penny's hands had been cuffed behind her back for almost 40 minutes, the gunshot wound to her arm left untreated. The paramedic was livid.

"Uncuff her right now!" he ordered Lauzon. Gounis was promptly loaded onto a stretcher and whisked away to hospital.

～

Paramedic Bruce Lewis arrived in the fourth ambulance to a report of an unconscious male. When he arrived on scene, he was guided into the dining room of the Brossard home. He saw a man lying face down on the floor, wearing only boxer shorts, his hands cuffed behind his back. The detectable odour of human feces wrinkled Lewis' nose. The man had obviously soiled himself.

Lewis examined the man, who appeared to be out cold, then ordered him moved into the ambulance. Two other police officers piled in as well. As Lewis continued his examination, he moved his fingers up to the man's eyes to examine his pupils. Lewis felt resistance in the man's eyelids when he tried to open them.

He's faking it, Lewis thought.

～

It became obvious almost as soon as Tessier's body arrived at Charles LeMoyne Hospital that there was nothing anyone could do to save him. Yan Marchand, a medical aide at the hospital, tried to revive him, but the nature of the gunshot wounds made his attempts futile.

And suddenly, the Laval Police Department found itself back to where it had been only 15 months ago—mourning the loss of one of their own.

～

On December 14, 2005, Laval Constable Valérie Gignac and her partner received a noise complaint at the apartment of François Pepin, a man already convicted of uttering death threats. He was under a court order not to possess any firearms, but a clause in the order allowed him to have a rifle for hunting.

When Gignac and her partner didn't receive a response at the door, they proceeded to try to kick down the door to gain entry. As Gignac was kicking, Pepin fired a shot through the door with a .338 hunting rifle. The high-powered round ripped through Gignac's bulletproof vest, killing her.

The loss was monumental. It spurred a change in tactics for Laval police when trying to gain entry. The workers' safety board in Québec, better known by its acronym CSST (Commission de la santé et de la sécurité du travail), was still investigating to see if Gignac and her partner had responded appropriately to the situation.

Thousands of officers from across North America turned out for Gignac's funeral. Now, not even a year and a half since her loss, which was still felt heavily throughout Laval's police force, the department had to bury another one of its comrades.

∽

Although Constable Stéphane Forbes had lost a lot of blood, hospital staff was able to quickly treat the wound to his arm. His condition was listed as serious but stable. So too was the condition of Penny Gounis, who had suffered a single gunshot wound to her arm.

At the hospital, it was left to RCMP crime scene technician Ed Yoshiyama to gather Tessier's belongings as evidence. The technician was on loan to the Québec provincial police force —the Sûreté du Québec (SQ)—that had taken over the investigation into the shooting. SQ detectives had sequestered the officers who had taken part in the raid to question them. Other officers were also questioning Forbes and Penny Gounis.

Tessier's bloodied shirt, emblazoned with the Laval Police Department crest, his bulletproof vest, his pants and his belt bearing his badge—No. 523—were all placed in paper bags. At the foot of the stretcher that the paramedics had used to transport Tessier to the hospital, both medical aide Yan Marchand and Yoshiyama found a baseball cap also emblazoned with the police logo. It went into the paper bag as well. Neither man noticed a total absence of blood on the cap.

Once stripped of potential evidence, Tessier's remains were placed in a locked room, guarded by two police officers.

~

By the time the fourth ambulance had reached the hospital, Basil Parasiris was conscious. And he was talking.

"How is the police officer?" he asked in English.

The question came suddenly for Constable Jacynthe Gaumond and her partner Constable Jihane Bouhid—neither of whom were fully bilingual—who had both escorted Parasiris to the hospital. In response to Parasiris' question, Gaumond informed him that he was under arrest for the murder of a police officer. Bouhid began to read out Parasiris' Charter rights, including the right to silence and the right to consult a lawyer, but Parasiris kept on talking.

"The officer is dead? Oh my God. I just killed a police officer," he said.

Bouhid continued to read Parasiris his rights. Parasiris asked about his wife and kids, and about the other police officer who'd been shot. He then turned to the officers and asked a pertinent question.

"What were you guys doing there?"

Neither officer responded. Gaumond made notes as Parasiris continued to talk, but she later stated that French was her mother tongue and that she was not bilingual, nor was Bouhid. Paramedic Bruce Lewis, who was still in their company, did speak English and acted as a translator. Initially, Parasiris declined his right to speak with a lawyer.

"I thought someone was coming to kill me," Parasiris said. Gaumond then re-cuffed Basil's hands from behind his back to the front of his body.

And Basil Parasiris buried his head in his hands and cried.

∽

Officers and civilians throughout the community, province and country reacted with shock that yet another police officer had been shot in the line of duty. Laval police chief Jean-Pierre Gariepy personally made the rounds of his detachment to deliver the news before making himself available to the media.

"I would say that our people are in a very deep shock. I would say a very heavy shock," said Gariepy. "Sometimes…it's like if you flip a coin. You get lucky or it turns out to be the other way. This morning it turned out the other way."

The rest of the raid was a success. The remainder of the warrants resulted in the arrests of five individuals—Nikolaos Xanthis, Constantine Xanthis, Kosta Katsiousleris, Hari Katsiousleris and Emmanuel Maroudis—all charged with a variety of drug trafficking offences. But the net result of the raid was overshadowed by Tessier's death. Condolences came in from across the county, including the highest levels of government.

"My heart goes out to the family, friends and colleagues of this brave officer who gave his life in the line of duty," Public Safety Minister Stockwell Day (Conservative) stated.

The police, however, said little about the raid, what its purpose had been and the person they had in custody. Using a land titles search, the press was able to establish that the home at which the raid occurred was owned by a Billy Basil Parasiris and his wife Penny Panagiota Gounis. It was not until a few days later that Parasiris was positively identified in the shooting death of Daniel Tessier. In all, Parasiris was charged with four different offences—first-degree murder in the shooting death of Daniel Tessier, attempted murder of Constable Stéphane Forbes, firing a gun with intent to wound Forbes and endangering Forbes' life by discharging a firearm.

Basil Parasiris was quickly transferred from the custody of the Laval Police Department to the SQ, who ordered him held at the Rivieres-des-Prairies Detention Centre. With Penny Gounis still in hospital, the children were handed over to family members for care.

With the death of Valérie Gignac still so fresh in their minds, the Laval force set up counselling services for all the officers affected by Tessier's death.

"Life goes on," said SQ member Gilles Falardeau. "Even if a police officer is lost, even if a police force is shaken by a second murder, police must look at their ability to follow calls."

The funeral for Daniel Tessier was scheduled for Friday, March 9, at St. Vincent de Paul Church in Laval. In the meantime, members of the public who wished to express their condolences were allowed to do so through an email address. The media was denied access to Laval headquarters. By noon on Monday, March 5, over 400 email messages were received. The force also planned a public service on Thursday, March 8, for those who wanted to pay their respects.

∼

Later that week, Parasiris made his first court appearance in Longueuil, represented by lawyer Frank Pappas. Family members blew kisses to Parasiris and waved from the gallery.

Parasiris was arraigned on the four charges, returned to custody and ordered to appear again on April 16.

In most murder cases, suspects and their attorneys choose to invoke their right to silence and cling to it like air. In this case, however, Pappas stepped outside the courthouse after the hearing and conducted a lengthy interview with the press in which he conveyed his client's perspective on what had happened.

According to Pappas, Basil had been woken up by his wife in the middle of the night because she heard a noise in the house. Basil, he said, had awoken in a panic.

"If he would've believed it was the police, do you think he would have taken them on?" Pappas said, who went on to state that the police found nothing of value inside the home after the raid. "There was no body, no drugs, no large quantities of firearms. They might have found one or two pills of Viagra that he didn't have a prescription for. This guy's no terrorist.

"If it had been some gratuitous shooting, where some gang member or someone walked up to a cop and just shot him, I would never defend him. I believe this guy feared for his life and family, that's why he did what he did."

Pappas acknowledged that his client had a licence for a handgun, but was not supposed to keep it loaded. "He should pay for that. But my client acted responsibly and is absolutely innocent."

He also pointed out the actions of Basil's 15-year-old son as proof of his client's frame of mind. "Do you think that if they knew they were police officers they'd call 911?" Pappas asked rhetorically.

The fireworks weren't just found outside the courthouse. There was also more drama emerging from the Parasiris' home. Several media outlets were given access to the home for television footage and then used the video to try to re-create in news broadcasts what might have happened inside. While a member of the Parasiris family would have had to give permission for the video to be shot, only the reporter appeared in the footage which featured the blood-stained floors and walls of the home. Police officers everywhere were outraged.

"It's the blood of a police officer who was just doing his job and died on the scene," said Sherbrooke officer Paulin Aubé, vice-president of the Federation of Municipal Police Officers.

Laval police chief Jean-Pierre Gariepy issued an open letter to the media protesting the move. "At a time when [Tessier's] family and colleagues are in mourning, a series of assumptions are being presented to the public as though they were actual evidence," he wrote.

~

Approximately 2000 to 3000 police officers from across Canada, including some from Vermont and a few United States border guards, descended on Québec for Tessier's funeral on March 9. Even Forbes received a temporary pass from the hospital to attend the service.

In −13°C weather, row upon row of police officers marched behind the funeral cortege as it wound its way through the streets of Laval. During the two-hour ceremony, which was simulcast to a nearby theatre at College Laval campus for the guests who could not fit into the church, Tessier's widow and one of his daughters shared their pain with the gathered throng of mourners. Forty-two candles, representing Tessier's age, illuminated the church. As the camera panned over Tessier's casket, draped in the Laval flag, every officer at College Laval leapt to their feet to pay tribute.

"Never could I imagine that someday my heart would break in two under the weight of the pain, the anger and incomprehension," Dominique Lapointe told the crowd, who responded with a standing ovation.

"I used to say that I wanted you all wrinkled, taking you to a whole bunch of activities with Maman when you retired," said Veronique, 12. "I wanted you to see the children of my children."

At the end of the service, Tessier's cap was given to his parents, and his badge to his daughters. The Laval flag draped over his coffin was folded and presented to Dominique, who in turn passed it to the Laval police force in honour of their service.

Outside, as the hearse waited, every officer stood at attention and saluted as Tessier's remains were loaded into the back and carried away.

~

With little information about the raid forthcoming from the police, the press started to dig further. Court documents obtained by the *Montréal Gazette* finally shed some light on what exactly was found at the Parasiris residence during the raid. Officers had uncovered a .357 Magnum revolver, four plastic bags containing an unidentified white or powdered substance, accounting ledgers, 17 cell phones and pagers, as well as $2000 in cash, a computer and computer disks.

Four other items were also found at the scene: the battering ram used by the police to make entry into the home, which was found on the second-floor balcony, and three 25-calibre bullets.

Defence lawyer Pappas stated that Basil owned the Ruger .357 Magnum, which was licensed and legally registered. Pappas had encouraged Basil to co-operate with authorities, which he had already done, telling his side of the story in a videotaped statement over the course of 12 hours immediately after the shooting.

On Monday, April 16, Basil was charged with eight new counts, all related to four firearms seized during the search, which were identified in other court documents. At the same hearing, Pappas submitted a summary of the arguments he would be using to try to secure bail for his client. It was a daring move. The bail hearing would be heard in Québec Superior Court, not at the provincial level, because the Superior Court automatically deals with cases of first-degree murder. Pappas' move was seen as a long shot—no one accused of killing a police officer in Canada had ever been granted bail.

Four days later, on April 20, Basil's bail hearing began in Superior Court. The justice presiding over the hearing heard testimony from both sides. The police testified that Tessier had been the second of five officers through the door, and the two were responsible for securing the upstairs. Blood-spatter evidence indicated that Tessier had been shot just as the master bedroom door swung open. The first bullet, fired from a .357 Magnum revolver, struck Tessier in the face and nicked his carotid artery, wounding him fatally. The second hit him in the arm and travelled to his heart, also a fatal wound. He was struck a third time while falling, then a fourth time in the foot. The fourth shot, however, had not come from the .357. The bullet was a 9 mm, fired by one of the officers in the raid.

Tessier, according to testimony, had been wearing a police-issue ball cap, a bulletproof vest with the word "POLICE" printed in large letters on the front and back, a Laval police polo-style shirt with crest and a badge affixed to his belt. All of the officers had shouted "Police!" when they entered the home.

The Crown also introduced evidence that Basil had confessed to shooting Tessier despite being warned of his right to silence.

"No matter. I have killed a police officer. I took somebody's life…" he had stated, along with, "I'm sorry. I heard a bang, somebody screaming. I freaked out."

The blood-spatter evidence also indicated that Tessier and Basil were no more than seven feet (two metres) apart when Basil opened fire. All tolled, three police officers fired 14 rounds during the gun battle, while Basil fired four times. The fourth bullet from Basil struck Constable Stéphane Forbes. The bullet that ended up in Tessier's foot came from the same gun that had fired the bullet that hit Penny Gounis. The gun was linked to Sergeant Nathalie Allard, who had been thrown off balance when Serge Lauzon backed into her during the firefight.

Pappas brought on some extra help for the case in the form of attorney Jacques Larochelle, known in Québec for defending Hells Angels biker gang head Maurice "Mom" Boucher. The pair argued that their client had been just as confused as the police officers outside his bedroom door, such as Serge Lauzon, who had fired at the wrong door. The defence presented evidence that showed it was not clear whether the word "POLICE" on the front of Tessier's bulletproof vest had been visible—the words can be covered up by a strip of cloth, and no one could remember whether or not Tessier had removed it. Lauzon also testified that when he dragged Tessier away from the firefight, he had pulled him across the floor on Tessier's stomach.

According to Forbes, he remembered shouting "Police!" when he and the other officers first entered the home, but he couldn't recall if the team had continued shouting it as they made their way up the stairs.

Parasiris took the stand and even admitted to the court that he had been trafficking in drugs for about three years to make up for a financial downturn in his life. He also told paramedics on the day of the shooting that he had been drinking and using cocaine the night before. The police had later found less than one gram of cocaine and two grams of marijuana inside the home.

On Monday, April 23, Superior Court Justice Jean-Guy Boilard rendered his decision—Basil Parasiris could be released on bail—the first time in history an accused fingered for killing a police officer had ever been granted release. The key turning point in the decision, however, had little to do with the raid itself and everything to do with the original warrant. According to Justice Boilard, the police were not justified in using a battering ram to execute their search warrant, and the warrant did not grant them permission to enter the home in the late night or early morning hours.

Basil was freed on two $100,000 bonds that were posted by his sister and cousin. He was ordered to obey a 7:00 PM to 6:00 AM curfew and had to live with family while awaiting trial.

Three days later, free from detention, Parasiris gave a statement.

"I'm really, really sorry for what happened. I honestly thought it was a home invasion or something."

~

One year later, on April 1, 2008, it was announced that the case would be decided during a six-week jury trial. The Crown and defence would convene on May 5, 2008, for pre-trial hearings, all of which would be subject to a publication ban, and jury selection would take place on May 13 with the intent of conducting a bilingual trial. The Crown prosecutor would be Joëlle St. Germain. Frank Pappas had since left the defence team, leaving the case in the hands of Jacques Larochelle and another attorney, Dominique Shoofey. The justice hearing the case was Guy Cournoyer, a bit of a celebrity in that he had served as special counsel to the commission conducted by Justice John Gomery into the Liberal sponsorship scandal.

The issue of the search warrant continued to dog the Crown, even before the trial officially began. During the pre-trial hearings, the warrant was central to the discussions that took place, and in the end, the defence scored a major victory. Justice Cournoyer ruled that the dynamic entry warrant was invalid. It was, Cournoyer said, abusive and violated Basil Parasiris' Charter rights against unreasonable search and seizure.

"The use of force was not justified under the circumstances because the case did not establish that a [regular search warrant] would bring about the loss or imminent destruction of evidence," the justice ruled.

The ruling effectively hamstrung the Crown in several different ways. It meant none of the Crown witnesses could say why they were even at the home in the first place. They could not mention the words "drug raid," nor could police officers from the drug and morality unit state they were members of that department. Parasiris' own confession at the bail hearing—that he had been trafficking in drugs for three years—was also inadmissible, as were the items police found, such as the drugs, the accounting ledgers detailing a drug trafficking operation and the 17 cell phones and pagers. The scope of the trial was strictly limited to the shooting and whether or not Basil Parasiris had been acting in self-defence when he shot Daniel Tessier.

Six men and six women were selected to hear the evidence of the first-degree murder trial of Basil Parasiris, which got underway on Wednesday, May 20, 2008. Basil entered a plea of not guilty to all four counts. Both sides admitted there was no issue of identification in this case; Parasiris was not denying that he shot Tessier.

"This Crown's case is not a whodunit case," St. Germain said.

The Crown told the jury they could expect to hear from 30 witnesses, including the eight officers on the scene, a ballistics expert, a pathologist and other crime scene technicians.

"Like a puzzle, all the pieces have to be put together before you reach a verdict," St. Germain told the jury in her opening remarks.

Photographs, specifically of the crime scene, Tessier's clothing and his body, dominated the first day of the trial. Dominique Lapointe wept as photographs of her dead husband's body were displayed to the court. Ed Yoshiyama, the RCMP crime scene technician on loan to the SQ was among the first to testify, detailing how he collected Tessier's clothing from the hospital then returned to the crime scene to gather all of the officers' firearms. According to Yoshiyama, Tessier's gun had a round chambered, but it was never fired.

During the cross-examination, Larochelle pointed to a photo of Tessier's bulletproof vest, which showed the word "POLICE" on the front covered in black material. Larochelle's strategy was obvious from the outset—he was trying to prove that Tessier had not been visibly identifiable as a police officer, which lent credence to Parasiris' claims that he thought he was being robbed.

There was also the issue of the baseball cap. Yoshiyama testified that he had retrieved the cap from the hospital, and medical aide Yan Marchand told the court the cap had been resting at the foot of the stretcher.

The trial became increasingly interesting as it moved into the next day. Bruce Lewis, the paramedic who took Basil to hospital, testified that Basil had told him he'd been drinking and using cocaine the night before. Lewis also said the defendant had stated he had been attacked a week before and that he had thought when the police came that it was someone else.

Larochelle decided it was time to grill Lewis.

"Did you hear him say, 'I killed him. The guy is dead. Oh no'?"

"No," Lewis replied.

"Did you hear him say, 'I didn't know it was a police officer'?"

"Yes, I did hear that," Lewis said.

Pathologist Annie Sauvage explained that the first two shots that hit Tessier had been fatal—the first entered through the jaw at close range, so close that gunpowder burns were visible on Tessier's face. The bullet then entered the neck and severed the carotid artery. The second bullet passed through his shoulder, into his chest and nicked the pulmonary artery, damaging his heart.

The witnesses who took the stand in the days following Monday, May 26, recounted the bungled raid in detail. Forbes recounted entering Stephanie's room when he was struck in the right arm and how he tried to keep her calm. Lauzon detailed his mistakes during the raid, while Allard testified about opening fire on the master bedroom when Lauzon bumped into her, knocking her off her feet. The tape of Allard's 911 call was played in court, in which the jury could clearly hear Lauzon demanding Basil give himself up, and Penny Gounis shouting "Oh my God!" in the background.

Larochelle confronted Constable Serge Lauzon about his actions after he arrested and handcuffed Basil. The officer admitted to grabbing Basil by the throat, threatening to punch him, then referring to him as "Mon hostie de sale." Lauzon even testified that, because he was not fully bilingual and Basil was not complying with his instructions, Lauzon demanded to be spoken to in French.

When asked point blank if he had also referred to Parasiris as "une hostie bloke" (a f****** Anglophone) while trying to get Basil to surrender. Lauzon replied that he wasn't sure.

Constables Gaumond and Bouhid recounted their experience with Basil at the hospital, reading from their notepads about his confessions despite being warned to remain silent and consult a lawyer. As every single witness took the stand, Larochelle honed in one key component—the baseball cap Tessier was supposed to have been wearing during the raid. The only proof of its existence to date in the trial had been its recovery at the hospital. None of the witnesses who had testified were able to say with any certainty whether or not Tessier had been wearing the cap, emblazoned with the Laval police logo, when he was shot.

The trial was not without its bizarre moments. One of the first officers to testify—an SQ detective—reacted with shock when Cournoyer ordered him to store his firearm outside the courtroom. On Wednesday, May 25, the justice was forced to remind the jury about the importance of "not nodding off" when it was noticed one juror repeatedly bowed his head and closed his eyes.

On Friday, May 30, ballistics expert Linda Vézina took the stand. According to her analysis, Tessier had been standing three feet (one metre) away from the muzzle of Parasiris' .357 Magnum. That calculation came from the arc of the gunpowder burns found on Tessier's face. When a gun fires, the gunpowder used to propel the round from its casing and out of the barrel follows it, spraying out in a wide pattern. The tiny, hot grains only fan out a certain distance, however. Because a .357 Magnum is more powerful than a 9 mm, the powder travels farther, meaning Tessier's face had powder burns on his lips and cheeks. The revolver was later found in the en suite toilet.

Three other guns were also found. What was never located was the third Magnum bullet that struck Tessier. Vézina explained that bullets fired from a Magnum tend to slow as they leave the body to the point where they can't even penetrate clothing. She also stated that it was possible the bullet fell out of Tessier's shirt when he was taken to hospital.

Jean Bergeron, a blood expert, testified the spatter of blood at the crime scene indicated that Tessier had been shot in front of the master bedroom, close to the door.

But the two expert witnesses had a strange story to tell, again revolving around the baseball cap. Although both Vézina and Bergeron had received the physical evidence shortly after the original shooting, the ball cap hadn't arrived for analysis at either of their labs until the month before the trial began, in April. Bergeron tested the cap for blood and found traces inside the lining, as well as on top, but in no great amounts. Larochelle asked him that if Tessier had been lying in a pool of his own blood, wouldn't there have been more of it on the cap?

"If it fell in the puddle, yes. If it fell farther, no," Bergeron replied, also acknowledging the blood traces could have resulted when the cap was placed in the same bag as Tessier's bloody clothing.

Vézina's testimony was even more puzzling. Despite her testimony that Tessier had suffered powder burns to his face, and that gunpowder had been found on his vest and polo shirt, her analysis of the baseball cap found no traces of gunpowder residue on it.

On Monday, June 2, Larochelle took the mystery of the cap a step further. Testimony at the preliminary inquiry had yielded evidence that Tessier had been wearing a black toque before the raid. A black toque was later found at the scene of the shooting and photographed, but none of the other officers said it was theirs. Neither Vézina nor Bergeron was ever sent the toque for analysis.

Larochelle called only two witnesses in Basil Parasiris' defence—Basil and his wife Penny. Basil, who testified first, told the jury about how he thought he was the victim of a home invasion. He said he'd been "fooling around" with Penny, then taken a sleeping pill. He awoke when he felt Penny elbow him in the ribs.

"The wife elbows me in the ribs and said, 'There's somebody in the house. The kids. The kids. Do something.'"

In response, Basil grabbed his .357 from the closet, at which point he said he could hear something akin to a stampede out in the hall.

"My kids were on the other side [of the hallway]. I had to do something."

He also added, "I soiled myself, I was so scared."

After shooting Tessier, Basil stated he saw the word "police" on Tessier's shirt as he fell.

"I started screaming, 'I didn't know it was the police.'"

As the bullets flew, Parasiris hid behind the door. He dumped the gun in the toilet, and when the shooting stopped, he crawled out on his hands and knees.

In her testimony, Penny said that the sound of the battering ram knocking down the door woke her up. "The third [bang] was really loud. I never heard anything like it."

She could hear shouting in the hallway but never heard anyone say the word "police." As Basil went for his gun and started shooting, Penny said she went to hide in the bedroom closet and that was when a bullet struck her in the arm. She was handcuffed and left without medical attention for almost 40 minutes before she requested an ambulance.

Larochelle had one last surprise for the jury, but he waited until closing arguments on Monday, June 9, to present it. Repeating his belief that Basil had been acting in self-defence when he shot Tessier, who was not identifiable as a police officer, Larochelle also suggested that Tessier had been wearing the toque and not the ball cap that no one seemed to remember.

At that point, Larochelle pulled a heavily stained black toque from a bag and showed it to the jury, asking if anyone could think it was stained in anything but Daniel Tessier's blood.

"The Crown is not interested in knowing if the toque was Daniel Tessier's. It places the perfect integrity of the Crown in doubt," said Larochelle.

In response, St. Germain simply asked the jury to con-
sider whether or not Parasiris' actions had been reasonable. He
did, after all, have three guns in his bedroom closet and one
hidden in the kitchen. According to St. Germain, Parasiris did
not assess the situation before opening fire.

"He chose not to check who was on the other side of the
door," St. Germain said, adding that Parasiris simply could have
called 911.

On Tuesday, June 10, the jury was sequestered until they
came back with a verdict. Before they left, Justice Cournoyer
issued his instructions—they could find Basil Parasiris guilty of
first- or second-degree murder, manslaughter, or they could
acquit him if they believed he acted in self-defence. Before the
jury was sent out, defence lawyer Larochelle pointed out that
the Crown had not successfully proved that Parasiris had tried
to kill or injure Stéphane Forbes, nor had the Crown proved
that he even knew Forbes was in the house.

Cournoyer agreed and acquitted Basil of the three
charges pertaining to Forbes, leaving only the question of Tessier's killing in the hands of the jury.

The first day passed with no verdict. On the second day,
everyone came rushing back to the courthouse as the jury
requested to speak with the judge, but it was only to listen to
recordings of his instructions, as well as Parasiris' and Penny's
testimonies. Two more days passed before the call came at

around 4:00 PM on Friday, June 13 that the jury had reached a verdict.

The courtroom was packed. The only notable absence was Tessier's widow, Dominique Lapointe. The foreman stood to deliver the verdict.

"Not guilty."

The announcement stunned the crowd. Basil seemed to be in disbelief, while Penny shouted, "Oh my God!" Within moments, Parasiris hugged his attorneys and left the courthouse without giving any kind of statement.

"He's relieved and satisfied by the decision of the jury. It was a difficult case for everyone," defence lawyer Dominique Shoofey told the press afterwards.

St. Germain announced that a committee would review the chance of an appeal, which would have to be filed within 30 days. On July 11, the Crown announced that after "profound analysis," they had decided not to appeal.

The reaction from the policing community was palpable.

"We deplore that no criminal responsibility was laid after the death of Constable Daniel Tessier," said Denis Côté, president of the Union of Municipal Police Officers. "We want every firearm in the country registered and a crackdown on black market firearms that are bought and sold."

Laval police chief Jean-Pierre Gariepy was also livid.

"There's only one person whose fault it is and that's Basil Parasiris. He's the one who pulled the trigger. He's the one who shot Daniel Tessier. He's the only one who's responsible for the death of Daniel Tessier. So if there's someone to blame, he should look at himself in the mirror."

According to Gariepy, Tessier's widow felt "...like we do. It's very hard. It brings back [memories] of a year ago."

Gariepy then asked the media to leave Tessier's family alone.

Basil Parasiris later gave an interview to the *Montréal Gazette*, lashing out at the police for resurrecting the idea after the trial that he was drug dealer in order to smear his name.

"It didn't affect the jury...but this was [something that affected] public opinion, you know?"

Basil Parasiris was forced to sell off the Golf-O-Max to pay for his defence, as well as his home. On September 9, 2008, Parasiris' lawyer Dominque Schoofey announced that her client would plead guilty to some of the remaining weapons charges stemming from the firearms the police recovered during the raid. One of the charges carries a mandatory one-year prison term. Schoofey acknowledged that Parasiris would likely serve jail time as a result of the plea. She also stated that the Crown and defence were not able to come to joint resolution and asked the matter to be pushed back to January 22, 2009, which was approved.

Shortly after the verdict, the workers' safety board in Québec announced a probe into the killing of Constable Daniel Tessier. It will likely be completed in the summer of 2009.

Since the verdict, the Laval police department has decided that only ERT teams will conduct dynamic entries.

Chapter Five

Constable Christopher Worden

Killed: *October 6, 2007, Hay River, Northwest Territories*

Accused: *Emrah Bulatci*

Charges: *First-degree murder; three counts obstruction*

Status: *Awaiting trial*

~

Friday, October 12, 2007

Ordinarily, the television newscasts in Edmonton seldom interrupt their regular broadcasts unless the breaking news is extraordinary. But this was no ordinary day in Alberta's capital city. At approximately 5:00 PM, the TV images started to flash across the community, thanks to a news helicopter, which members of the Edmonton Police Service (EPS) and the RCMP had been trying to keep away from the area all afternoon. The overhead footage, slightly jittery, showed heavily armed tactical officers escorting a man from a southwest Edmonton townhouse. His hands were behind his back. He was wearing only track pants and no shirt.

The man was taken from one patrol car to the next, then was put in an ambulance where a convoy of police vehicles, with overhead and emergency lights flashing, took up escort both in front of and behind the ambulance. The news helicopter stayed with the ambulance for most of its journey, which ended at the University of Alberta. Little was known about the condition of the man.

The assembled throng of media back at the townhouse quickly started to disperse. The word was out—a press conference had been scheduled at the northside headquarters of the RCMP in Alberta, known as K Division. Photographers and reporters from local print, radio and television news agencies, as well as some representatives of the national media, frantically packed up their gear and roared off to the fenced-off compound to make it to the briefing on time. It wasn't the story they were after; everyone who had been on-site already knew what had happened. But they needed confirmation from the Mounties; they needed details; and they needed quotes and footage to wrap up their stories.

Shortly after 6:00 PM, a face now synonymous with the ongoing investigation, that of K Division media officer Corporal Wayne Oakes, stepped before the press and spoke briefly to the media, all jostling to get the best possible angle, the better shot. The television and radio stations, with their satellite trucks and units outside, broadcast the press conference live to air across the entire city. Oakes' words were light on details but confirmed what everyone in the room wanted to share with their audience. Oakes promptly ceded the microphone to Chief

Superintendent Fred Kamins, commander of the Mounties for the province of Alberta.

While Kamins expressed a "sense of relief" that the ordeal was over, few were interested in his exact words. It was all just colour. Reporters were already on their BlackBerries and cell phones, firing off confirmation of the news so that news anchors, announcers and websites could finally be updated with the news that residents in Edmonton, St. Albert, but most especially Hay River, Northwest Territories, had been anxiously waiting to hear for almost a week.

Emrah Bulatci, 23, the most wanted man in Canada, charged with the first-degree murder of RCMP Constable Christopher Worden in Hay River, was finally in custody.

Saturday, October 6, 2007

Glen Larsen, a longtime resident of Hay River, was fast asleep when an increasing volume of chatter from his police scanner woke him up shortly after 5:30 AM. As Larsen blinked the sleep from his eyes, his ears and brain finally connected, and he sat quietly listening to the voice of one of the Hay River RCMP dispatchers who kept calling out, almost desperately, without response.

"All she kept saying was, 'Please respond...please respond,'" Larsen later said. There was no reply.

Another resident, who asked to remain anonymous, was up at the same time, listening in on her scanner. Shortly after 8:00 AM, one of the worst, most dreaded calls came over the Hay River RCMP channel.

"They said, 'Officer down.'"

RCMP Constable Christopher Worden, 30, was a happy man, one week away from a much-anticipated vacation. He and his family were getting ready to fly to Ontario, to pick up his in-laws and then drive all the way back to Hay River in a motor home. Attached to the nine-member RCMP detachment of Hay River, the Ottawa native and former co-captain of the Wilfrid Laurier University Golden Hawks football team was strong, smart and a dedicated member of Canada's national police force. Christopher and his wife Jodie were relatively new parents, as Jodie had given birth to Alexis just eight months earlier.

Worden had wanted to be a member of the RCMP since he was in high school. He was accepted into training at Depot in Regina and, four months into his training, proposed to Jodie. After graduation, Worden was posted to Yellowknife, before moving on to Hay River. He and Jodie married in 2003. Almost four years later, Alexis was born, on February 6, 2007. The Wordens wanted to stay in Hay River for another three years and then had planned to transfer somewhere south.

Although Hay River dubs itself the "hub of the North" or "the port of the North," it is still a small town, despite the oil sands boom in northern Alberta and the lucrative diamond trade in the Northwest Territories. The town's population hovers around the 3600 mark, making the community small and its facilities even smaller. Located on the south shore of Great Slave Lake at the mouth of the Hay River, the town was starting to feel the negative effects of seeing so much of the industrial world pass through it. Expansion in the Northwest Territories meant a high demand for workers, which meant an even higher demand for everything else, including drugs.

Both the crime statistics and the stories of disgusted local residents told the story of the expansion of the drug trade into the Northwest Territories via the "port of the north." Data from Statistics Canada showed two disturbing trends—first, that the number of drug offences across the territory as a whole was more than twice the average of the entire country. More shocking still was the second trend—violent offences in the North were seven times as common as in other regions of Canada. The North, according to some experts, was an "untapped market" for the drug trade, and the police began to see organized crime trying to establish its roots. Over a five-day span in June 2007, members of the RCMP in northern Alberta and the Northwest Territories seized 1.25 kilograms of cocaine, as well as crack, magic mushrooms and marijuana headed for the North. They also seized a loaded handgun—severely restricted in Canada—and a total of $20,000 in hard cash.

Robert Halifax, a retired judge from Hay River, was getting fed up with the situation.

"A lot of kids tell me it's easier to get drugs than alcohol," he said. In fact, Worden, had recently given testimony in a trial about a quantity of cocaine he had found in a subsidized apartment building in 2006. The town was small, but the drug problem was big. And it was up to nine RCMP officers at the Hay River detachment to try to keep the problem under control. Given the escalating crime, it was surprising there hadn't been a murder in the entire territory for almost two years. Up until that point, there had been four per year, on average, between 2001 and 2004.

It was Worden's parents' 34th wedding anniversary, but by the time he arrived home in the early morning hours of October 6, the milestone was probably one of the furthest things from his mind. He had just finished his shift and was on call for the night, eager to grab a least a little sleep before his phone rang calling him out to some problem or another. He kissed both his daughter and wife and went to bed.

Shortly after 5:00 AM, the phone rang. Worden pulled on his uniform and took off into the night on a call about a problem at the same subsidized housing complex where he had found the cocaine one year earlier.

Three hours later, the other members of the Hay River detachment found him lying in a wooded area beside the building, suffering from multiple gunshot wounds. By 8:30 AM, doctors at the hospital pronounced Constable Christopher Worden dead.

Whether its subjects want it to or not, news travels fast. And news that a member of the RCMP had been killed while on duty shot across a country already sensitive to the perils police face every day.

Only two years earlier, a gunman named James Rozko shot and killed four members of the RCMP at his Mayerthorpe property before turning his gun on himself. The crime seeped into the public consciousness and generated a greater respect not only for the RCMP, but also for all city and provincial police forces across Canada.

The press release sent nationwide about Worden's death that Saturday took little time to find its way onto the desks of weekend reporters and the Internet sites of larger newspapers, promising that more information was forthcoming.

The RCMP acted quickly once Worden's body was found. Crime scene investigators taped off the wooded area behind the apartment building on Woodland Drive while units in Hay River and Yellowknife erected roadblocks. By the evening of October 6, however, it was clear that whoever they were looking for was already gone. Almost as quickly as they went up, the roadblocks came down.

On Sunday, October 7, the police released more information to the public. At 2:00 PM, the Hay River RCMP held a press conference with Chief Superintendent Tom Middleton, the commanding officer of G Division, the RCMP headquarters for the Northwest Territories.

"Words can never convey the sorrow that is felt when a member of the Royal Canadian Mounted Police pays the ultimate sacrifice," Middleton said. "Our thoughts and prayers are with everyone who has been touched by this."

Middleton released a few details about what had transpired in the early morning hours on Saturday. Worden had been dispatched to a call shortly after 5:00 AM. His last radio communication indicated he was entering the address identified in the call, and additional units were dispatched when Worden stopped responding on his radio. He was finally located in a wooded area outside the building and rushed to hospital, where he was pronounced dead.

Despite media queries, Sergeant Larry O'Brien, who took over the press conference, refused to elaborate on the exact nature of the call Worden was responding to, nor why Worden was sent on the call alone.

"The investigative team has identified a suspect and are actively pursing the avenues of investigation. To protect the integrity of the investigation, we are unable to share further details at this time. The investigators believe there is no immediate threat to the community of Hay River....RCMP procedures call for backup to be used in certain situations. At this time I can't speak to the nature of the complaint, so I can't tell you if policy was applied," said O'Brien.

As the day wore on, the RCMP released more information. They not only had a person of interest or a suspect in mind who they needed to track down, but they also knew exactly who they wanted to talk to. Late Sunday, the RCMP issued an arrest warrant for a 23-year-old man named Emrah Bulatci. The warrant reflected that a charge of first-degree murder had already been laid against him. The media release advised that Bulatci also went by the name of Justine Elise. Police issued a warning that Bulatci was considered armed and dangerous, and that no member of the public should try to approach him if they saw him. They also believed Bulatci had fled the Hay River area. They noted known addresses in Edmonton and St. Albert, a suburban community northwest of the city, and said that Bulatci was somehow connected to a 2004 grey Ford Expedition SUV, bearing licence plate LEC 010.

Even though the issuing of the warrant and the laying of the charge were made public, the police did not release a photo of their suspect to the media. A press release announcing the arrest warrant and charge listed a description of Bulatci, saying he was approximately 5 feet, 1 inch, weighed 134 pounds and had blond hair and blue eyes.

A four-block area around the Woodland Drive apartment building in Hay River was sealed as the police collected evidence. Twenty-five Mounties from Alberta and the Northwest Territories descended on the town of Hay River to relieve the nine members of the local detachment. Residents told the media that the subsidized apartment building, surrounded by mobile homes and townhouses, was often a spot for trouble. Problems with drugs and alcohol were frequent.

But what also came out was the community's respect for Constable Worden. Stephanie Rose, a local resident, had once worked with a local women's shelter. Worden stopped by frequently to help make the women feel more comfortable, and he made extra patrols of the area whenever Rose asked.

"And on his way home, he would be tired, but he would always drive by and let me know how things were looking outside."

Worden's father-in-law also shared a few thoughts with the media.

"He wouldn't do anything else," said John Lamers. "He loved his job."

On Monday, October 8, Jodie Lamers Worden, now a widow, made an appearance in front of the media, supported by her parents and in the company of eight-month-old Alexis.

"As a husband and father, Chris is irreplaceable," Jodie said, reading from a prepared statement. "While we're still in shock and disbelief that he's no longer with us, it gives us strength to know that we have the support of a nation that recognizes and appreciates the ultimate sacrifice Chris and other men and women have made for them.

"We thank you for your thoughts and prayers and ask that you grant us privacy as we begin to deal with the loss of our beloved Chris. Thank you."

It seemed as though half the media was trying to figure out exactly who Christopher Worden was and what had happened to him, while the remaining half turned their eyes towards the suspect charged in his death, Emrah Bulatci.

That same morning, press reports featuring interviews with Bulatci's family members and former acquaintances were springing up in papers across Alberta.

"He is a nice guy, he is very family oriented," his brother told one reporter, asking not to be named. "I'm in shock."

The brother confirmed that Emrah had recently been living in St. Albert with his girlfriend and their baby daughter. Emrah Bulatci grew up in High Level and had been working on the drilling rigs for several years.

The brother had spoken with Emrah on Sunday night. Emrah claimed he wasn't aware that a warrant had been issued for his arrest.

"I still don't know why he would go [to Hay River]. His kid is in St. Albert or wherever he's living now. I don't think he's going to take a 14-hour drive or however long it is and leave his three-month-old baby," said the brother.

Emrah's father, Erdogan, who ran a barbershop on the main street in High Level, said he wouldn't encourage his son to turn himself in.

"If he did something, I would tell him to go to the cops, I don't think he did something like that," Erdogan said, adding he hadn't seen his son in almost a year.

"He usually calls me when he needs money or he's in trouble. Then he just calls me, but I never heard anything from him."

Few people in the town of High Level were surprised by the news of the warrant and the charge sworn out against Bulatci.

"It doesn't shock me. He has had altercations with the law before," said one former teacher.

"He's been a bad apple for a lot of years. The courts had many opportunities to leave him locked up and they chose not to," said one High Level resident.

"He's not some cuddly guy who had a baby," said another woman.

As the reporters continued to pry, more details about Bulatci's background came to the surface. The suspect was born in Turkey, and his family had come to Canada in 1989 when he was only four years old. He had an extensive criminal record. In total, Bulatci's record contained 25 criminal charges dating from 2003 in four different communities.

One of the most notable incidents that came to a light was an arrest on February 7, 2007. Members of the Edmonton Police Service (EPS) gang and drug units noticed suspicious activity near a vehicle parked in a commercial shopping district on 137 Avenue and St. Albert Trail in Edmonton. When they raided the vehicle, they seized $7000 in cash. That led them to a home on 153 Avenue and 137 Street, where a search of the home allegedly yielded another $36,000 in cash, as well as 13 ecstasy tablets. Bulatci was arrested with two other individuals, both of whom allegedly had links to the Hells Angels and Crazy Dragons, organized criminal gangs with a presence in Edmonton.

Bulatci was charged with possessing the proceeds of crime over $5000, possessing the proceeds of crime under $5000, careless storage of ammunition and two counts of breaching a recognizance. Despite strong objections from police, Bulatci was granted bail, albeit after he forked over $20,000 in surety. Such large bail amounts in Canada are exceedingly rare. It didn't matter, however, because on August 31, 2007, the Crown withdrew all of the charges except for one breach of recognizance count. Bulatci pleaded guilty and was fined $1000.

One month after the February 2007 arrest, members of the St. Albert RCMP arrested Bulatci and charged him with two counts of breaching his previous arrest recognizance, driving without a licence and obstruction by giving a false name. While the St. Albert RCMP asked for Bulatci to be remanded into custody, the justice of the peace at the time ordered his release on $3000 bail, which Bulatci paid. That case is still before the courts.

Earlier court records showed Bulatci had faced outstanding charges of dangerous operation of a motor vehicle and disqualified driving in Grande Prairie. In High Level in 2005, Bulatci was found not guilty of robbery, two counts of aggravated assault, one count of theft over $5000 and one count possession of stolen goods. He was, however, convicted on one count each of possession of a weapon, uttering threats and breaching probation, for which he received a 10-month intermittent jail sentence (meaning he could serve the time on weekends), one year's probation and a 10-year firearms ban. Previous charges included a 2004 conviction for assault in High Level, for which he was fined $300, and charges of possession of a controlled substance and failure to produce a driver's licence, for which he was fined $875.

The RCMP issued a "Be On the Lookout" (BOLO) warning to all of its compatriots in Western Canada. The RCMP was still not sharing much information regarding Worden's death, nor did they release a photo of their suspect or Bulatci's whereabouts.

The national and daily media went to bed that night waiting for the RCMP to turn up Bulatci's trail. Little did anyone know that the trail led right under their noses and that they would be three days too late in picking it up.

All of the media, that is, except for one paper.

Weekends in St. Albert, population 57,000, can be boring, especially when you're a news photographer and there's not much going on, and especially when it's Thanksgiving long weekend and everyone else is cooped up inside their homes feasting. But Lyle Aspinall, a photographer with the twice-weekly *St. Albert Gazette*, was driving around town in the company of his girlfriend Denise, looking for something to photograph.

Aspinall was doing circles through the city when he heard a call come over his portable scanner, asking for a "marked presence" at a local church. Curious, Aspinall drove by the church and instantly found himself looking at what is for St. Albert an uncommon sight.

"We went to the church and we saw a parking lot full of uniformed police, all in SWAT gear with machine guns and dogs and a bomb robot," said Aspinall. "They didn't look anxious, they just looked to be gathering."

Aspinall was ordered out of the parking lot, but he took up a spot on a nearby sidewalk and started taking snapshots. Despite all his efforts, none of the police on scene would tell him what was going on. After another hour, the assembled police squad packed up and moved out. Aspinall returned to the *Gazette*'s office, filed his photos and made a quick call to editor Sue Gawlak about what he'd seen. He then hopped back in his car to make some more rounds.

Again it was the scanner that tipped Aspinall off as a hurried voice asked for a drop-off at a home in St. Albert's

Akinsdale neighbourhood. Aspinall rushed off to the address and again his instincts paid off. Police had taped off a neighbourhood home and were milling around in SWAT gear, donning submachine guns and facemasks. Uniformed officers stood watch on the lawn, clutching shotguns. When Aspinall tried to approach, he was warned off. He backed off to a public sidewalk and started shooting with a longer lens. He also pulled out his cell phone and dialed the number for *Gazette* court and crime reporter Ryan Tumilty.

As a displaced Ontario native far from his family, Tumilty had nowhere else to be on the holiday Monday other than work. He was just filing a couple of stories for the paper's Wednesday edition when Aspinall called to tell him what he was looking at. Tumilty promptly set off for the scene.

"He [Aspinall] called me and said a home in Akinsdale had police tape up, two officers on the lawn with shotguns and a tactical team or part of one sitting in an SUV in the driveway," Tumilty said. "The crime tape up was a red alarm, but the shotgun and the tactical team were huge."

The officers on scene were visibly wary about the pair being on scene, but no other media had yet arrived. The only people Tumilty could see inside the house were police officers. He spoke briefly with a neighbour, who said there were always young people coming and going from the house.

Then something unexpected caught the reporter's eye.

"There were two vehicles in the driveway—a crappy-looking Ford Aerostar van and a very nice-looking silver SUV" said Tumilty.

Tumilty admits that what he saw "didn't register right away." He rifled through all of the press releases he had printed off pertaining to Worden's death. Finally, the light bulb went on. He circled back and had a closer look at the SUV.

"A vehicle they were looking for was a silver SUV, a Ford Expedition with big chrome wheels, and when I turned around and looked at the SUV, it fit every one of those requirements. The only way to know for sure was to walk up beside the house and take a look at the back, at the licence plate, which is what I did."

The light bulb in Tumilty's head exploded. The plate on the back of the SUV—LEC 010—matched exactly the plate number the police had said they were looking for.

"That's when we figured out that Emrah Bulatci's SUV had showed up in St. Albert," said Tumilty.

The disadvantage of working for a twice-weekly community newspaper is that any news item worthy of significance will likely be picked up by the daily newspapers before a community paper can publish it. Tumilty spoke again with his editor at the *Gazette* that evening.

"We thought it was great that we had it, but there was no way we were going to end up writing the story ahead of everyone else."

Tuesday, October 9, 2007

The next morning, the Edmonton daily papers were full of information about the Worden case. The police revealed that Worden's service automatic had been found on his person, meaning he likely hadn't been shot with his own gun. The RCMP had conducted searches in and around High Level, suspecting that because Bulatci grew up there, he might have family and friends willing to hide him. The consensus seemed to be that Bulatci was likely still in Alberta, but that he might have even fled into the wilderness.

With the *Gazette* due to publish on Wednesday, Tumilty spent all day Tuesday trying to confirm what he'd found. Every call he made to the media liaison officer in the Northwest Territories came back busy. He contacted members of the local St. Albert RCMP detachment, who promptly refused to comment. "They wouldn't touch it with a 10-foot pole," Tumilty said.

Finally, Corporal Wayne Oakes, the media liaison for K Division in Edmonton, was able to give Tumilty the information he needed.

"Oakes confirmed the information for me. He told me that they did know it was his [Bulatci's] SUV; they believed pretty strongly that he had it in Hay River; they were confident he fled the scene in it. He said what they didn't know was how it got from Hay River to St. Albert."

Then Oakes uttered the words that every reporter working on a big story loves to hear.

"He told me I had something that no one else had. So we ran with the story," said Tumilty.

Wednesday, October 10, 2007

By Wednesday morning, the media knew two things that they hadn't known the day before. They finally knew what Emrah Bulatci looked like. After a four-day wait and much pestering by news agencies, the RCMP finally released a photo of the suspect late Tuesday. The police found itself on the defensive, trying to explain why it had taken so long to get the picture out to the public.

"Privacy legislation restricts the information we are able to release," Oakes said, a comment that later came back to haunt him.

The police also knew what had transpired in St. Albert two days earlier. Both Edmonton daily papers updated their websites, crediting the *Gazette* with the initial story. By 10:00 AM on Wednesday, the phones at the *Gazette* were ringing off the hook as almost every news agency, local and national, called to try to get a copy of Aspinall's photo that was featured on the front page of the paper.

A member of the Emergency Response Team walks between two vehicles parked at a St. Albert home. The police had been looking for the grey SUV (left). (Photo credit: Lyle Aspinall/*St. Albert Gazette*)

That same day, a woman by the name of Shari Wynne started up a group on the increasingly popular social networking website Facebook, dedicated to finding Bulatci. By 4:00 PM that afternoon, 600 Facebook users had joined the group.

"I just wanted to get as many people as possible to see his face, just to get him caught as soon as possible," Wynne told the press.

Erdogan Bulatci, meanwhile, still refused to issue any plea to his son.

"Why should I call [the police]? Maybe they are lying."

Thursday, October 11, 2007

If they were trying to be quiet about the story, the EPS tactical team wasn't doing a good job of it. By Thursday afternoon, officers with body armour, sniper rifles and submachine guns, accompanied by a Grizzly armoured personnel carrier and a bomb robot, had cordoned off an inner-city neighbourhood in Edmonton, seemingly focusing their efforts on three houses within a three-block radius. The media instantly converged on the area, including Aspinall and Tumilty, who got a tip from a source about the pending raid.

Two men had already been taken into custody by the EPS for questioning. One of the men later told the press that he'd been visiting a friend in one of the homes when the police came for him. He denied having seen Bulatci.

"Even though we're all ex-cons, we don't believe in what that guy did," the man, identified as Chris, said. "None of us knew him, but even if we did, we told the cops that if we did see him we'd beat him down until they got there."

The police used a bomb robot to search the area, then set off a flash-bang grenade before making entry into one of the houses.

Aspinall, shoved off to one side with the rest of the media, watched the raid unfold.

"Four or five officers approached one of the homes, guns drawn, shields up, very protective, crouched down like you would see in a movie, and that was just a brief few seconds," Aspinall said. "We knew it was unsuccessful when they just came walking out, all relaxed."

Jeff Wuite, a spokesperson for EPS, told the assembled media that the tactical team had been deployed to assist the RCMP with a homicide investigation, but refused to say whether the investigation was connected to Worden's death. The inference, however, was obvious.

"You don't have to be a genius to put two and two together," Tumilty said.

Back at the *Gazette* office, Tumilty managed to secure an interview with a woman who lived in the St. Albert home the police had raided on Monday. The woman, who claimed to be the mother of Bulatci's girlfriend, shared some interesting information with Tumilty.

"She said she knew him well and he would never do something like this, and her heart went out to Constable Worden's widow," Tumilty said. "She also said the SUV had never left St. Albert that weekend, had been there the whole weekend. She never said anything about if Bulatci had been there with it."

Friday, October 12, 2007

The seventh day of the manhunt started off with a strange piece of information. The RCMP had, they claimed, some information stating that Bulatci might not actually be in Edmonton. In fact, the tip put him heading towards Prince Rupert, BC, in the company of a woman in a green or navy 2002 Ford Escape. The RCMP in Prince Rupert responded by setting up roadblocks in the area and questioning drivers. The source of the information, however, was cited as being "unreliable."

The RCMP also issued an updated description of Bulatci. They now listed his height as 5 feet, 3 inches, instead of 5 feet, 1 inch, his weight as 190 pounds and claimed he had dyed eyebrows and jet-black hair, cut in either a short buzz or spiky style. He was last seen wearing grey sweatpants, a black windbreaker, a white ball cap with blue stripes and white Nike runners with gold stripes.

Whether the RCMP in Edmonton believed the Prince Rupert tip or not, they still had other tips, and with the help of the EPS, they acted quickly. Early Friday morning, the police, acting on a tip that came in between 9:00 and 10:00 AM, contacted officials at Ormsby Elementary School in southwest Edmonton and advised them to put the school in lockdown. No children were allowed outside the school, and no one was allowed in. By 2:30 PM, six city buses had pulled up to the school and evacuated the students to another school, where their parents were asked to pick them up.

A pair of tactical officers arrived and quickly disappeared into the surrounding neighbourhood carrying sniper rifles. At approximately 3:40 PM, tactical officers set off a pair of flash-bang grenades in front of the Callingwood townhouse. More police started showing up, and as they did, the media followed. Aspinall and Tumilty received another tip from a colleague and quickly headed to the area. It was going to be tight. The *Gazette* was due to publish the next day, and Tumilty's story had to be in by 5:00 PM.

Shortly after the police arrived, two people were pulled from a nearby townhouse for questioning, but the police and the media stayed on scene.

"I remember someone saying, 'I got a hunch about this one,'" Aspinall recalled.

By 4:15, nothing else had happened on scene. Tumilty hopped in his car and raced back to St. Albert to file his story before deadline.

Aspinall stayed behind, waiting with all the other photographers in the distance. Just before 5:00 PM, there was a flurry of activity at the front door of the townhouse the police were watching. Aspinall brought his camera to his eye and started shooting.

"When the police came out, they were leading someone who looked an awful lot like Emrah Bulatci in the wanted pictures we were seeing."

Aspinall barely had five seconds to shoot, but of all the photos taken during that brief span, his shot of a shirtless man in track pants, his arms coloured a mysterious purple, turned out to be one of the sharpest. After cycling through his shots to make sure he had something usable, Aspinall called the *Gazette* office.

"He [Aspinall] said the police had just dragged someone who looked an awful lot like Bulatci from this townhouse. It didn't take long before everyone else was confirming that," Tumilty said.

The *Gazette* decided to hold the press run to allow time for Tumilty to attend an announced news conference at K Division headquarters and for Aspinall to file his best shot. The EPS revealed it had established contact with Bulatci inside the Callingwood townhouse through "intermediaries" who convinced him to surrender.

"We opened up the screen door and he came out," said Jeff Wuite, a spokesperson for EPS.

At the press conference an hour later, Superintendent Kamins, Alberta's top RCMP officer, addressed the media and confirmed that the police had their suspect, Emrah Bulatci, in custody. He had been escorted to the University of Alberta Hospital as a precaution. Kamins also stated, "At this point, no additional charges have resulted and the investigation is continuing."

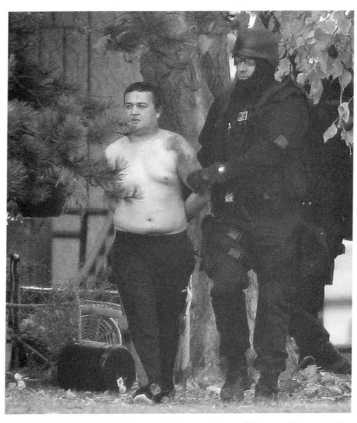

Emrah Bulatci is escorted from an Edmonton home following his surrender. He faces a charge of first-degree murder in the death of Constable Christopher Worden. (Photo credit: Lyle Aspinall/*St. Albert Gazette*)

"That was the end of that," Tumilty said. "They took a few questions, but they weren't getting into a lot of details. Kind of self-congratulatory...we got him."

~

Kamins, as it turns out, was wrong about no additional charges having been laid. Shortly after Bulatci's arrest, the EPS announced that one of the men who was pulled from the townhouse earlier Friday, Jarred Dale Nagle, had been charged with accessory to murder after the fact.

"It's in the context of aiding and abetting, if you will," Corporal Oakes said. The second person—a woman—was released without charge.

Kamins agreed that Bulatci had likely received some assistance during his seven days on the lamb.

"We had a lot of people out looking for him. I would be surprised if someone could do that themselves."

Oakes was facing a little heat himself, this time from the Alberta Privacy Commissioner, Frank Work, with respect to Oakes' October 10 statement that the RCMP had not been able to release Bulatci's photos because of privacy legislation.

"They may have had their reasons for not releasing it, but privacy should not have been one of them," Work stated.

Bulatci was placed on a six-day remand in order to ship him back to the Northwest Territories for a court appearance. In the meantime, another story fell out of the cracks of the Internet when Matt Galpin, 18, decided to start a group on Facebook entitled "Long Live Emrah Bulatci." When confronted by the media, the 18-year-old admitted he had been drunk, and he issued an apology.

"I regret ever doing this."

His father assured the public that his son's Internet access had been revoked.

"This isn't about free speech. It's about disrespect and poor taste," Jim Galpin said.

~

With their prime suspect in custody and another man charged, the RCMP could finally turn its attention to one of its most sombre duties—paying respect to one of its own. On Monday, October 15, a parade of RCMP officers dressed in their formal red serge accompanied the hearse carrying Worden's body down Sussex Drive in Ottawa towards Notre-Dame Cathedral Basilica. Hundreds filled the church, including little Alexis, dressed in a tiny Mountie tunic.

One by one, family and friends stood before those gathered and shared their memories of Constable Christopher Worden.

"Chris, you're one of the greatest guys we have ever known. Your heart, friendship and sense of humour are irreplaceable," said Constable Mike Carter. "What you have given us is beyond measure. You will never be forgotten and will forever be a part of our lives....Rest in peace, my friend."

The Canadian flag draped over Worden's coffin was later folded and presented to his family. A similar, smaller ceremony was held in Edmonton in the lobby of K Division beside the

Wall of Honour, dedicated to every RCMP officer who had been killed in the line of duty.

Back in Hay River, 300 residents attended a public meeting, calling for curfews, for parents to watch their teens more closely, for the town to deny subsidized housing to anyone convicted of a drug offence and for residents to watch for out-of-town licence plates.

Jodie Worden spoke at a memorial ceremony in Hay River on October 27. She said that drugs had killed her husband and that the community needed to fight back.

"Chris died because of the illegal drug trade. Please don't let his death go without meaningful consequences."

During an interview on CBC Radio, Jodie called on the RCMP to change its policies regarding single patrols in isolated communities, stating her husband might still be alive if he'd had a partner the night he was killed. Liberal public safety critic Ujjal Dosanjh took up Jodie's call, asking the RCMP to review its guidelines, which the force promised to do. It came back with a proposal that listed the specific calls for which backup would be required. It did not, however, establish any protocol for responding to calls after dark.

"They need to send two members to every call. That's just an officer safety issue," Jodie later said.

On Friday, November 23, 2007, media outlets in the town of Hay River reported police were searching the west bank of the Hay River with metal detectors. The search lasted the better part of two days. The RCMP stated it was part of the ongoing investigation. No details were released.

On December 13, 2007, Bulatci appeared in court in Yellowknife without a lawyer. He appeared again on January 25, 2008, this time with Laura Stevens on the record as his lawyer. No plea was entered.

Jarred Dale Nagle, the man charged with accessory to murder after the fact, was released on bail on December 17. He is expected to enter a plea on November 29, 2008, in Edmonton

In early February 2008, the RCMP announced that Bulatci faced three new charges, each one a count of obstruction. The RCMP alleged in the charges that Bulatci had asked associates of his to tamper with witnesses. None of those allegations has been proven in court, and the police released few details about the incident.

However, shortly after Bulatci's arrest, the media got a copy of the affidavit and arrest warrant charging Bulatci with first-degree murder in Worden's death. What they found, none of which has been proven in court, finally sheds some light on what happened to Constable Christopher Worden on Saturday, October 6, 2007.

According to the affidavit accompanying Bulatci's arrest warrant, Worden was called out at 5:03 AM about a possible suicidal man at a subsidized apartment building on Woodland Drive. Earlier that morning, two brothers—Patrick and Robert Lafleur—had gotten into a fight. Robert had punched Patrick, breaking his nose. Patrick left the apartment, and Robert called the police.

Worden radioed in at 5:31 AM, stating he was leaving his vehicle. It was his final radio call. According to the affidavit, he stopped at a local convenience store then went to the home of Patrick's aunt, Rachel Martel, who lived at 55 Woodland Drive. Martel was a person well known to the RCMP, according to the affidavit—she was scheduled to appear in court October 31 on charges of cocaine trafficking.

As Worden arrived, he saw three men leaving the residence, one of whom allegedly was Emrah Bulatci. The affidavit states that Bulatci and the two other men had been at the home, smoking marijuana, drinking and playing video games. The men were about to get in a cab when Worden allegedly pulled up and asked them what they were doing. The cab driver stated the man believed to be Bulatci put his hands on the trunk of the car as if to be searched, then ran as Worden approached. Worden took off in pursuit.

Patrick, meanwhile, had gone to his mother's house. Both were awake when they heard a series of gunshots. His mother—Nancy—phoned the police, and while looking out the window, saw a man running past, through the trees.

Another woman heard four or five gunshots.

At 6:30 AM, the RCMP dispatcher on duty phoned the detachment sergeant, saying Worden hadn't answered his radio for one hour. The sergeant responded to the scene, where a woman said she saw Worden chase a "fat man" into the forest. Patrick volunteered to accompany the police, more of whom were arriving on scene, and to show them where he had seen the man flee. The officers found Worden's car outside Martel's residence. And they also found Worden within the next hour. He had been shot four times in the neck, chest and abdomen, possibly with a 9 mm Glock handgun. RCMP officers use sidearms manufactured by Smith & Wesson.

An ambulance arrived on scene and took Worden to the hospital at approximately 8:00 AM. He was pronounced dead at 8:30 AM.

One woman, who had been listening to her police scanner throughout the whole ordeal, alleged that Bulatci and the two other men had been staying in town on and off throughout the summer and usually stayed at 55 Woodland Drive.

"They've been through here [for a week or two at time] all summertime at least, and they're not the only ones. But I guess you're never going to stop it because people want drugs. That's why people are hush, hush and let it be," the woman said.

∼

On January 28, 2008, a territorial court sentenced Rachel Martel, 43, to one year in jail plus two years' probation on one count of cocaine trafficking.

In early April, a community elder, confined to bed because of poor health, started a petition to get enough signatures to have the Hay River airport named after Christopher Worden.

"He never raised his voice. He was an intelligent person," said elder Joe Mercredi. "He talked to you like a human being."

By April 11, Mercredi had gathered several hundred of what he hopes will amount to 1500 signatures on his petition.

Bulatci has not yet entered a plea. On February 28, 2008, territorial court Judge Brian Bruser scheduled a preliminary inquiry for June 16, 2008. A preliminary inquiry is a hearing in which a judge decides whether or not there is enough evidence to substantiate a charge. Bulatci's hearing is expected to last two weeks. If ordered to stand trial, he will have to enter a plea.

According to a publication ban issued by Judge Bruser, the media will not be able to report any of the evidence presented at the inquiry. A second ban applies to a court order the Crown will be requesting; the ban makes it illegal to even report on what the order actually is.

On September 8, 2009, Emrah Bulatci appeared in St. Albert Provincial Court under heavy escort. Dressed in a prison-issue set of blue coveralls, with his hands cuffed and legs shackled, Bulatci pleaded guilty to three outstanding charges of obstruction of a police officer, breach of bail conditions and driving with a suspended licence. Bulatci spoke only once, uttering the word "guilty" when the charges were read. He was sentenced to 20 days in prison and fined $500.

Chapter Six

Constables Brock Myrol, Anthony Gordon, Peter Schiemann and Leo Johnston

Killed: *March 3, 2005, Mayerthorpe, Alberta*
Gunman: *James Roszko, 46—killed, self-inflicted gunshot wound*
Suspects: *Shawn Hennessey, 28; Dennis Cheeseman, 23*
Charges: *Four counts each first-degree murder*
Status: *Trial pending, April 2009*

∽

"No matter the era, it seems that children always want to grow up to be police officers—to wear the uniform, enforce the law, catch the criminal. There's a timeless appeal to this impulse. It reflects a young mind's growing understanding of right and wrong. It reflects a young heart's yearning to keep people safe and families whole.

"Years pass, children grow up, but for some the desire, the dream, remains. The idealism and fantasy of a child give way to the realism and determination of an adult. There are bad people in the world, and they do bad things. Someone must stand against them.

"Anthony Gordon, Lionide Johnston, Brock Myrol, Peter Schiemann: This was their dream. They dedicated themselves to standing up for what is good in our world, to serving their community, to protecting their neighbours.

"With their loss, we are left numb that a single act of hate has affected so many lives, caused so much grief, interrupted so much love. With their loss, there is a singular intensity to our mourning—those who have fallen have done so selflessly; those who have fallen have done so in service to a nation, to an ideal; they have fallen in service to us.

"We use the word debt to remind us of something owed. The people of Canada owe an untold debt to these four officers and to their families. We owe a debt to each and every woman and man who chooses to put on the uniform, to submit to risk, to face harm, to uphold the law. The presence here of so many police officers, from cities and communities across the continent, is a testament to the camaraderie and the devotion that thrives within the law enforcement community. The bonds forged by dangers shared are strong and they are everlasting.

"Most Canadians know these four constables only through media reports and the official RCMP photographs we've all seen on television and in newspapers.

It can be heartbreaking to look at those pictures, for in their faces there is youth, and in their expressions a solemn dedication to duty—a duty that would ultimately call for the greatest sacrifice.

"But look closer, and in their eyes there is pride. Look closer, and on one, even the hint of a smile. How could they not have been proud? They were members of our national police force. They were Mounties. To wear the uniform of the RCMP is to dedicate oneself to feats of courage and nobility of purpose. These four young men, alive in the early summer of life, rest now in the serenity of God's embrace. They are mourned by neighbours, and by a nation. Their memory will be eternal. So too will our gratitude."

–Prime Minister Paul Martin
Mayerthorpe memorial service, March 10, 2005

March 2, 2005

3:20 PM

Two bailiffs sat in a black truck on a country road, waiting. In their hands were the documents they needed to repossess a vehicle. According to the order—issued by Kentwood Ford—the company had been unable to verify the credit information of the man who had purchased the white 2005 Ford F-350 truck. The owner also hadn't answered or returned any of their phone calls. Consequently, the dealership was taking back the truck.

The bailiffs were quite a distance from the dealership. The property they were looking upon was in the hamlet of Rochfort Bridge, just outside the town of Mayerthorpe, Alberta, population 1700. The small municipality, with its farmers, and oil and gas workers who passed through, is approximately 170 kilometres from Edmonton. That's where Kentwood Ford was located. And that's where the truck was being returned.

The two bailiffs got out of their truck and surveyed the farm property in front of them. Roughly three quarter sections (480 acres) of open land stretched as far as the eye could see. That is, until, the eye came to the level of the gate that barred entry to the property. What the bailiffs could see, however, was a small trailer home and an enormous Quonset hut, silver metal from top to bottom, dominating the skyline with its half-moon shape.

Despite their presence at the front of the gate, the bailiffs got no response from the occupant inside, which, in the repo business, wasn't that unusual. Mark Hnatiw and his partner scanned the scene in front of them but noticed nothing out of the ordinary. Finally, a short man—all of 5 feet, 5 inches and 160 pounds—walked into view, wearing a black ball cap, blue jeans and a dark jacket. They tried to get the man's attention, but surprisingly, he refused to look at them and walked directly across their path on the other side of the padlocked gate into the Quonset hut. Annoyed, Hnatiw reached inside the black truck and honked the horn to try to get the man's attention.

The men heard a sudden rustle of feet and the unmistakable barking and growling of a dog. It actually turned out to be more than one dog, as two Rottweilers came running out of the Quonset, jumping, barking and snarling at them from the other side of the gate. The bailiffs retreated to their truck. Hnatiw started to get an uneasy feeling. He and his partner had no idea who this man was, but he was acting strangely, all because of a truck. Hnatiw grabbed his cell phone and dialed the phone number for the local RCMP detachment to request assistance in executing his order.

Just as he was finishing the phone call, Hnatiw looked up. He watched as the man started driving south through a gate on the property in a truck that looked like a white 2005 Ford F-350. Then the truck backed up, heading in the direction of the bailiffs. The man inside stopped the truck, got out and opened a chain-link fence. As he returned to the truck, he turned towards the bailiffs.

"F*** off!" he yelled, then hopped back in the truck and took off north.

It didn't take long for the RCMP to arrive. Two cruisers showed up at the scene mere moments after the man had taken off in the truck. The bailiffs may not have known the man they were dealing with, but the RCMP members sure did. It was James Roszko.

One of the cruisers immediately took off in the direction he had fled, hoping to apprehend him. Unfortunately, with Roszko's head start and his knowledge of the terrain, the officer was unable to catch up with him. He did come across a group of girls who had seen the truck—they were riding on horseback, and the truck had actually sent them scrambling. The truck then went through a nearby fence. But there was no sign of the truck and no sign of Roszko.

Back at the farm, with a police presence backing them up, the bailiffs cut the lock off the front gate and drove towards the Quonset hut, hoping the truck they'd seen flee the property wasn't the one they were supposed to repossess. The police officers confronted the angry Rottweilers with pepper spray, sending the once vicious dogs fleeing. With no other vehicle matching the truck's description in sight, the bailiffs stopped their truck near the Quonset, got out and went inside the hut. Within moments, they were back outside, beckoning the officers to join them.

The interior of the hut was cavernous, but it was full of vehicle parts, tools and machinery. It was the parts that caught the bailiffs' attention. Throughout the hut, vehicles—some newer, some older—sat in various states of disrepair. There was a newer Ford truck with the doors and interior removed. Closer inspection also revealed a GMC Sierra pick-up truck. The only thing out of the ordinary was that the truck's Vehicle Identification Number (VIN) had been removed, making it illegible and untraceable. An all-terrain vehicle sat nearby, as did pieces of a motorcycle. Scattered among the vehicles were bumpers, fenders, dashboards and new tires, as well as an assortment of tools and a massive generator—later revealed to be stolen—with a value of $30,000. The hut bore all the markings of a "chop shop," street language for a location where stolen vehicles are disassembled and the parts sold on the black market.

But the vehicles weren't the major find. Probing deeper into the Quonset hut, the bailiffs and police came across something they didn't expect to find—20 mature marijuana plants, as well as approximately 260 other plants in varying stages of growth, and all the hydroponic equipment required to grow the illegal drug in Alberta's inhospitable climate. The police also found a barrel outside the Quonset, stuffed with several kilograms of dried marijuana leaves.

The officer in charge, Corporal James Martin, quickly ushered everyone out of the Quonset and back to their vehicles. The Rottweilers had returned, and the police pepper sprayed them again. This time, the hounds fled into a nearby granary. To keep them confined in the metal structure, one officer used a cruiser to push a doghouse against the granary's opening, effectively pinning the dogs inside.

The officers were going to need a search warrant, but they were also going to need some help from their colleagues. The Mayerthorpe detachment was a small one and, while perfectly capable of policing the rural community, it didn't have the special resources needed to investigate a chop shop or a marijuana grow-op. The joint Edmonton Police Service (EPS) and RCMP Green Team in Edmonton, who worked together to track down and weed out grow-ops, was called in, as was a two-member team from the Auto Theft Unit at the RCMP's K Division headquarters in Edmonton. The Green Team officers were sent out first—the marijuana had an estimated value of $300,000. The Auto Theft Unit would come by the following morning, once the Green Team was finished with the scene.

Corporal Martin started preparing a search warrant that would permit them access to the property as mandated by the courts. Even though Roszko had fled the scene, Martin wasn't convinced he was truly gone.

"Roszko fled the scene in a white truck and is believed to be in the area of the property," Martin wrote. He knew Roszko. Everyone in the detachment knew Roszko. And they knew there was little chance he would simply saunter away.

James Roszko was a lot of things in life—a menace, a stalker, a gun lover and a convicted, untreated sex offender and pedophile. Growing and harvesting illegal drugs was news to everyone at the detachment. But it didn't surprise them.

~

James Roszko was born on November 8, 1958, to William (Bill) and Stephanie Roszko. James' father had come to Canada from the Ukraine in 1929 as a child and married Stephanie in 1950. From the year the couple were married until the end of the decade, Stephanie gave birth to a child almost every year.

Of the eight children in the family, James was the second youngest. He was adored as a boy, seen as an average student and polite, but one who seemed to easily slip out of trouble. James' older brothers were strapped viciously for any transgression, but none of them ever remembered James being on the receiving end of the leather switch.

"He became an expert at getting his way," said one brother. While the brothers had to do chores every day, James was exempt from that responsibility, which annoyed his siblings at the time.

In truth, neither one of James' parents paid much attention to him because of the couple's volatile relationship. Bill was old-fashioned, insisting on attending services at the Ukrainian Catholic Church every Sunday, whereas Stephanie was more modern in her thinking. As the '50s rolled into 1960, Bill had a revelation—the world was going to end in 1961. It wasn't a private revelation either; he preached it wherever he went and to whomever happened to come by for a visit. There was always a Bible at his side, and he was known to go so far as to preach his vision of Armageddon in local bars.

Bill's behaviour embarrassed Stephanie, to the point that in January 1960 she tried to commit suicide, but she was saved after her stomach was pumped. In 1969, Bill started accusing Stephanie of cheating on him. Stephanie asked for a divorce, but Bill refused to grant it for the sake of maintaining the family structure. In February 1970, Bill went to work at a sawmill camp. When he was gone, Stephanie left the home for that of another farmer, Martin Posser, taking the youngest daughter Mary-Ann and seven of the Roszkos' cows. When Bill returned, he immediately petitioned for divorce. The court hearings became ugly, as Stephanie claimed that Bill had slapped her, got drunk and forced intercourse on her. She also claimed that on one occasion he even threatened her with a gun. Bill denied it all, even after the divorce was finalized.

James was caught in the middle of the family drama. He went to live with Stephanie and her new husband and then went to live with his father. James refused to go to church, but Bill allowed it so his boy wouldn't go crying back to Stephanie. At the age of 14, James started dealing with his problems by smoking weed. One of his siblings later found his stash and informed Bill, who reported James to the police.

At school, James was a loner with few friends. One teacher—Mary Anne Neal who taught Roszko Grade 9 in 1973—said she saw in James a boy who was just looking for some attention.

"I knew Jim as a kid reaching out, as a kid wanting somebody to care for him," Neal said. "I wonder if things would have turned out differently if he had had help. My heart went out to that kid."

Finding James' stash was the first in what would become a litany of petty and ever more violent crimes as he grew up. Shortly after being accused of stealing a gun, James was removed by social workers from his father's home and placed with a local family, which he quickly left to stay with his mom. Stephanie, however, was having problems of her own. Though she'd married Martin Posser in 1972, she divorced him in 1978. It was a trend that would continue for years. She remarried in 1978, left that man in 1984 for another, and then left that man for another farmer in 1989.

James dropped out of school in Grade 11 but kept getting into trouble with the law. At the age of 17 he was caught stealing from a hardware store and received a fine and probation. He went to work on the rigs in the Northwest Territories as well as in the U.S. But he couldn't seem to stay out of trouble. He allegedly put sugar in the gas tanks of RCMP vehicles in 1976. And in 1979 he spent almost two months in jail for a rash of petty crimes. His hatred of the RCMP began to grow, and he came to sincerely believe that the police was picking on him.

While working on the rigs, James was known as a hard worker, but he also demanded loyalty from his friends. When he found out that one of his friends was co-operating with the authorities on a perjury charge Roszko was facing, he drove the friend to a quiet area and shot him in the foot. Neither was charged in the incident.

James returned to his mother's home in 1983, at which time his criminal deviancy took a disturbing and sickening twist. On one day that year, James, now 24 years old, had his shirt off and was suntanning in the presence of a 10-year-old boy. According to court documents and records, James suddenly took off his pants and started fondling himself. He asked the boy if he could see his penis, then reached out and touched it. James threatened to beat the boy if he told anyone what had happened.

That first incident was the beginning of an ongoing predatory relationship with the boy. Over the years, the assaults escalated to mutual masturbation and oral and anal sex. James would give the teenager money in exchange for sexual favours. When the youth started liking girls, James became jealous, but the abuse continued. It wasn't until the teen's family moved away in 1990 that the abuse finally stopped.

James preferred the company of teenage boys—there was no visible female presence in his life aside from his mother, who lived across the land James had purchased in 1985. He was often seen hanging out in his truck outside the local high school, watching the teenagers come and go. He recruited a small gang of followers, plying the underaged boys with beer and letting them use his growing collection of guns out on his property. The prized item in the collection was a Heckler & Koch .308 semi-automatic rifle. Illegal in Canada, the rifle could fire rounds as quickly as the shooter could pull the trigger. James had smuggled the gun across the border after a work stint in the States. James and the boys would shoot at milk jugs and an old washing machine on his property. Roszko was an expert shot, able to peg targets from hundreds of yards away.

The police were aware of Roszko's love affair with guns; everyone in the community knew James never left his property without a gun of some kind, whether in his truck or on his person. Between 1993 and 1998, based on information from the community, the police searched his house on three separate occasions looking for automatic weapons, especially the Heckler & Koch. All they came away with was a 9 mm handgun and a shotgun, neither of which was returned to Roszko. He still had plenty more that he kept buried in and around his property, and still others that were in plain sight. Anyone who got too close to his property was often chased off by a warning shot.

His love of guns kept James in the good graces of his teenaged crowd, giving him access to more victims. James began a sexual relationship with another underaged teen, this one 17 years old. While together on a road trip to Utah, James told the youngster he was dying of cancer and wanted to see a penis before he died. He then pulled out a handgun and held it to the teen's head. He also started rebuilding a truck for the youth and showered him with gifts and money. On another occasion, James appeared unexpectedly at the teen's home with a gun and threw him on the bed. A struggle ensued, during which Roszko's gun discharged and the teen pulled a kitchen knife and stabbed Roszko in the jaw. Rather than turn him in to the police, the youth accompanied James to the hospital, then stayed at James' place for several days.

Rumours of the relationship started to circulate around town, turning James into even more of a social pariah, and the treatment he received enraged him. In October 1993, he asked the 17-year-old to kill Brendan Duff, one of many who were telling everyone that Roszko was gay. Horrified, the teen refused and avoided James as much as he could. The teen then started dating a girl, which infuriated Roszko even further. In December of that year, Roszko tracked the teenager down at a movie theatre in Whitecourt and forced him into his truck. When they arrived at James' property, instead of going to the trailer, Roszko drove into a field and pulled a shotgun on the youth. He handed the teenager a pair of handcuffs, then started beating him, asking him if he was telling people that Roszko was gay. Unsatisfied with the answer, Roszko drove the teenager back to his trailer and forced him to pose for a series of sexually revealing photographs, saying he would pass them around if he told anyone about Roszko's sexual preferences.

At the end of the demeaning photo session, Roszko demanded oral sex and then released the teen, who started walking down the highway to school. By pure chance, an RCMP cruiser pulled up, and the officer took the youngster back to the detachment, where he voluntarily gave a statement. Based on the statement, the RCMP swore out charges against Roszko of pointing a firearm, counselling to commit murder, unlawful confinement, possessing a weapon for a purpose dangerous to the public peace, assault with a weapon, breach of recognizance and obstructing justice.

These weren't the first serious offences Roszko had ever faced. A few years earlier, in April 1989, James became incensed when he learned that the County of Lac Ste. Anne had changed his younger brother Doug's school bus route in a way that added 30 minutes to his travel time. Roszko personally tracked down Donald Szybunka, the supervisor of student transportation for the county, boxed him with his truck and threatened to kill him if he didn't change the bus route back. Szybunka laid charges against Roszko, resulting in conviction and a $200 fine.

Shortly after his December 1993 arrest, while in custody Roszko received an unexpected visit. The first teen he had sexually assaulted, who had been 10 years old at the time the abuse began and was now a grown man, came to visit him in cells. The two were engaged in a lawsuit as the man had lent Roszko money to buy cattle and equipment back when the victim had been a teenager, and James had never repaid the loan. During their brief meeting, James told him that he was going to change, and that satisfied the man.

As the trial date approached with respect to James' second sexual assault victim, James went to work, threatening and beating up witnesses, even going so far as to chase the teen in his truck. James' hatred of the RCMP continued to grow; he started following officers around town, then their wives, and filed frivolous complaints against almost every member of the Mayerthorpe detachment. He constantly listened to his police scanner at home, writing down the names and vehicle numbers of every officer in the surrounding detachments. He even told a friend, "If they ever come for me, I'm going to take a hell of a lot of them with me."

James' pressure tactics worked. Just as Roszko's trial was about to start, the teenager skipped town. The Crown issued a warrant for the teen's detention, located him, brought him back, then held him until the night before the trial, at which time they decided to let him spend a night at home with his family. But by the next morning, the teen had disappeared. As a result, the entire case against Roszko fell apart, and he was acquitted.

Seeing the case unravel weighed heavily on the mind of James' first victim. From what he could see, James hadn't changed at all. Although he was now an adult and could choose to leave the matter behind him, the man felt compelled to do something. He went to police with his story. Charges of sexual assault and sexual touching were laid against Roszko, who employed the same tactics as he did in the previous trial. He hunted the man down and pepper sprayed him in a hotel room, for which he was charged with five more counts, two of which were stayed and three of which were withdrawn. Roszko's actions didn't work this time. In March 1994, Roszko was found guilty of sexual assault and sexual touching and was sentenced to five years in jail. The conviction, however, was overturned on appeal and a new trial ordered.

Roszko was now so reviled in the community that he had to start doing business in Barrhead. Teens taunted him and vandalized his property, forcing him to put up spike belts at the entrance and "No Trespassing" signs everywhere. The signs and belts, however, weren't enough to stop a pair of adversaries on September 9, 1999. Nate Watson and Bob MacDougall, who had been drinking at a local bar, decided to stop by Roszko's property to send him a message. Unfortunately, James was waiting with a gun. He forced MacDougall to the ground, tied him up and threatened him. When Watson appeared out of nowhere, Roszko opened fire, grazing the man's arm and face with a shotgun round. James loaded the two men into their truck and offered to take them to the hospital, but instead he drove deeper and deeper into his property. Frightened for his life and that of his friend, one of the men grabbed the nearby shotgun and started pounding on James' head with the stock, striking him approximately 10 to 12 times, leaving Roszko in a bloody heap. The pair escaped, but all three men ended up being charged by the police. Roszko's charges were stayed, while Watson and MacDougall were acquitted at trial.

"He should have been an abortion," Watson later said.

The year 2000 brought another trial for James, but one he was already familiar with. His first conviction for sexual assault was overturned by the Alberta Court of Appeal, and a second trial was eventually scheduled. This time, Roszko wasn't so lucky. He was found guilty again and sentenced to two and a half years in jail, as well as prohibited from having firearms in his possession. There was no appeal—Roszko was incarcerated at the Bowden

Institution just outside Calgary, Alberta. Even in jail, he refused to admit he had ever done anything wrong. He kept a low profile during his jail stint, as child molesters within the prison hierarchy are viewed as the scum of the criminal world. His status as a sex offender didn't stop him from displaying his trademark temper whenever someone in a position of authority came near him.

"It was like a light switch," said one guard, referring to Roszko's propensity for being totally calm one minute and flipping out the next.

James refused any kind of treatment as a sex offender while in prison, and he was never granted early release. He was set free in December 2001 under statutory release, when two-thirds of his sentence had expired, but he was still on parole for the duration of his sentence. After six months, James was re-arrested and thrown back in jail for refusing to co-operate with his parole officer. The Correctional Service of Canada later issued a report stating that assessing Roszko's risk to the community was "impossible." James was released from prison in August 2002. Two months later, his parole expired, and the criminal justice system had no way of keeping tabs on him.

The sexual assault convictions created a division within the Roszko family. After he was found guilty at his first trial, the family were almost equally split over whether or not they wanted anything to do with James. Half of the family, including his mother, continued to support him, while the other half refused to have anything to do with him, including his father. Although

James lived only a few miles from his father and a couple of his brothers, he went years without seeing them.

"As far as I'm concerned, we're related by name only," his brother John said.

The family members he did keep in touch with, he helped when he could. He showed up at their homes with Christmas presents, helped pay bills when money was tight and often spent hours talking on the phone with his youngest sister, Josephine (Jo) Ruel.

Now back in the community, James learned to keep his head down for the most part, but that didn't stop him from doing his best to antagonize the police. He would speed past cruisers well in excess of the speed limit, goading them to chase him and doing his best to lose them, which he always did. He continued to keep updated notes on which officers from which detachments were in which cars, worked which shifts and were assigned to which cell phones. Still, his behaviour made him a frequent target of the RCMP. He was ticketed for speeding, and once for having windows on his truck that were tinted too dark. Each time he was pulled over he displayed his characteristic temper, exploding in front of the officers and complaining about harassment. His complaints against individual officers continued, even though every single one was considered frivolous.

Aside from the occasional traffic violation, James did little to attract police attention. The last entry on his criminal record was in 2004 when he was charged with two counts of mischief—a pair of election enumerators, who didn't know any better than to avoid Roszko's property, drove up to his front gate and ran over a spike belt he had laid across the entrance. The result was a couple of flat tires.

By February 2005, James Roszko had been charged with a total of 44 offences during his lifetime, but had been convicted on only 14 of those charges. According to a Crown review of his file in October 2005, Roszko had been flagged in the criminal database as a potential "dangerous offender." One more conviction for a serious crime would be grounds to trigger proceedings to have him declared a dangerous offender, a classification that would allow the Crown to imprison him indefinitely—the harshest penalty available under the Criminal Code of Canada.

It never happened.

March 2, 2005

6:30 PM

With Roszko's truck gone, and with him nowhere in sight, Mark Hnatiw and his partner taped a notice of seizure on Roszko's trailer home and left the farm. They had been at the property for three hours and felt there was little chance the truck they were after would return anytime soon.

RCMP members from the Mayerthorpe and nearby Whitecourt detachments were called to assist with the search of the property and the search for Roszko. By 7:55 PM, a justice of the peace had sworn off on the search warrant that Corporal James Martin had prepared, which gave the police the authority to turn the property upside down over the next 24 hours.

Martin made one quick call to K Division, discussing the approach the Auto Theft Unit would take when it arrived on scene the next day with the non-commanding officer (NCO) in charge. The first priority was getting the search warrant to Roszko's property as well as looking for James Roszko. Martin started interviewing officers who were the most familiar with Roszko, asking them where they thought he might be and what he could be doing. The detachment put in place a plan that allowed them to search nearby buildings for their suspect and secure the scene at the property. Roughly 45 minutes after obtaining the search warrant, Martin, with six officers in tow, returned to Roszko's farm. A couple hours later, members from the Edmonton Police Service-RCMP Green Team arrived on scene and searched the Quonset and the rest of the property for more evidence that would add to the marijuana grow-op case. Officers from Mayerthorpe and Whitecourt were dispatched throughout the area to continue the search for Roszko, while a tow truck began hauling seized vehicles off his property. As a matter of safety, one officer was assigned to accompany the tow truck driver at all times. A member of the Edson Forensics Identification Unit, roughly 30 minutes away, also attended to assist with the investigation.

Despite the hefty police presence and several reports of sightings of Roszko, which turned out to be false, there was no sign of him on the property or anywhere else nearby.

March 3, 2005

At approximately 3:30 AM, the EPS-RCMP Green Team concluded its work, carrying off their haul of 280 marijuana plants, dried marijuana and growing equipment to Edmonton for further analysis and identification. The auto theft officers weren't due to arrive for another five hours. As the drug officers sped off, Martin assigned Constables Anthony Gordon and Lionide (Leo) Johnston to guard duty, telling them to keep an eye on the property overnight. Martin then left the property.

Some officers on scene, however, felt uneasy about the situation.

"When I left, I told the boys to make sure everything's clear because he's watching us," Mayerthorpe RCMP Constable Julie Letal said later.

The weather that March night was mild, and the peace and quiet of the surrounding countryside was punctuated only by calls over the police radio and the constant barking of the two dogs trapped inside the granary. Constables Gordon and Johnston spent their time walking around the property, armed with their 9 mm Smith & Wesson handguns, with access to a .308 rifle in one car and a shotgun in the other. The RCMP had chosen one of the best possible sets of hands to place those weapons in when they recruited Johnston to the force.

~

Leo Nicholas Johnston was 34 years old, newly married and one of the best shooters in his detachment. His twin brother Lee was also a member of the RCMP, and both were part of a prestigious club within the force—they each had "shot crowns," meaning they had shot perfectly during firearms training, not only with their sidearms but with a rifle as well. The distinction allowed the two Lac La Biche natives to sew a pair of badges on their serge uniforms—one of a crossed set of pistols, the other a crossed pair of rifles.

Lee and Leo were good shooters, but they were also good people and exceptionally driven individuals. The brothers had raced motorcycles competitively growing up, doing so at a professional level. They were also talented athletes, especially at badminton, which the pair played together when they attended high school in St. Albert, Alberta.

It was Leo's drive to master his motorcycle that led to a near-fatal accident in September 1997. During a feature race at the Calgary Race City Speedway, Leo collided with a second rider at a speed of 130 kilometres per hour. The collision sent Leo flying from the bike, the impact leaving him with broken ribs and severe head injures. The young man of Métis descent spent one week in a coma before awakening. Amazingly, he recovered completely from his accident. Four years later, Leo joined the RCMP and, after completing training at Depot in Regina, Saskatchewan, was posted to Mayerthorpe.

"Leo was the kind of person who lived his life and didn't sit in the back watching everything go by," said Art Mackenzie, owner of Calgary Speedway.

He had married the love of his life—Kelly—in late 2004. The couple hadn't even gone on their honeymoon yet.

Working with Leo Johnston that March night was 28-year-old Constable Anthony Fitzgerald Orion Gordon of the nearby Whitecourt detachment, a few minutes drive from Mayerthorpe. Gordon was a happy man; not only was he doing a job he loved, but he was also going to be a father—again. His wife Kim, a nurse at the hospital in Whitecourt, was expecting their second child. The pair already had one young son. Gordon's career with the Mounties had been relatively brief, three years in total. He was born in Edmonton and joined the force in Red Deer. After graduating from Depot, he was posted to the Whitecourt detachment on October 15, 2002. The town of 8700 people was a good place to live, with plenty of activity to keep Gordon and his fellow members busy. Gordon also loved the outdoors, especially fishing and riding his snowmobile, so the posting in Whitecourt was perfect for him. In an interview with a newspaper shortly after being posted, Gordon had told the reporter that he had wanted to be a police officer ever since Grade 1, when a Mountie visited his school.

"It got my wheels spinning, and that was my goal ever since," he said.

∽

The cool March morning seemed to stretch on like an eternity as Johnston and Gordon patrolled the Roszko property, but there was no sign of anyone or anything, except for the dogs still locked in the granary. As the last tendrils of the night began to fade away and the sun rose on the eastern horizon, the Mounties decided to do something about the dogs. They laced some meat with sedatives and dropped it into the granary.

Finally, at approximately 9:00 AM, a vehicle pulled up to the property and out hopped two new faces, one of those faces newer than the other. Constables Peter Christopher Schiemann, 25, and Brock Warren Myrol, 29. Despite their ages, it was Myrol who was the junior of the two officers, having only graduated from Depot a month earlier and reporting to Mayerthorpe shortly afterwards. This day, March 3, was Myrol's 17th day on the job.

Born in Outlook, Saskatchewan, Myrol had been working as a security guard and studying towards an undergraduate arts degree at Red Deer College when he decided he wanted to join the RCMP.

"I wanted the opportunity to work with people and be able to make a difference," he told the *Mayerthorpe Freelancer* when he reported for duty.

He gravitated naturally towards music as his entire family seemed to have a talent for it. He sang and played guitar, even composing a few works himself. The gentle refrains of his music stood in contrast to his other major accomplishment—a black belt in karate. Besides joining the RCMP, Myrol had also taken a larger plunge in life. On Christmas Day, he proposed to his girlfriend Anjila, who responded with an emphatic yes.

Although one of the youngest members of the detachment, Constable Peter Christopher Schiemann was the grizzled veteran of the group of four men when it came to policing. He had been posted to Mayerthorpe in December 2000, right out of Depot, and hadn't been transferred anywhere else. Born in Petrolia, Ontario, Peter had moved with his family to Stony Plain, Alberta, where his father Don worked as a Lutheran minister as well as the district president for the Lutheran Church for Alberta and British Columbia. Peter had attended Concordia University College in Edmonton, where he sang in the choir and regularly attended chapel services at the school. When he graduated in 2000 with a sociology degree with a psychology minor, Peter immediately applied to the RCMP.

"I think his commitment to be there for others led him to have a desire to enter into the service of the RCMP," said Concordia president Richard Kraemer.

Peter Schiemann was actually mentoring Myrol, but the two had more in common than they thought. They had recently decided to start attending church together.

On the morning of March 3, 2005, Schiemann had dressed in plainclothes, on duty but tasked with heading into Edmonton to pick up supplies for the detachment. When word of what was found on Roszko's farm reached him, Schiemann contacted Myrol. The rookie officer had never seen a marijuana grow-op before and was eager to get a look at it. The pair joined Johnston and Gordon, with Myrol in full uniform and Schiemann in his plain clothes, just as the last of the meat had been fed to the dogs inside the granary.

At 9:15 AM, two more police officers with the K Division Auto Theft Unit pulled up to the property, one of whom was Constable Steve Vigor, a longtime RCMP member and trained tactical member. All four officers approached the vehicle and traded handshakes and greetings with the pair from Edmonton, then pulled out the search warrant and gathered around to review it. With their plan set, Myrol, Schiemann, Johnston and Gordon walked towards the Quonset hut.

The four men entered the hut and disappeared inside while Vigor and his partner put on coveralls and started gathering their tools.

Moments later a shot rang out.

～

Vigor looked up as a bang echoed through the Quonset hut nearby. He wasn't entirely sure what he'd just heard. But within heartbeats the bang was followed by another, then another and a rapid succession of others, and in that moment, Constable Steve Vigor knew exactly what he was hearing. Someone had just opened fire with a rifle. And the gunshots were coming from inside the Quonset hut.

CONSTABLES BROCK MYROL, ANTHONY GORDON, PETER SCHIEMANN AND LEO JOHNSTON   *233*

Vigor yelled to his partner to make sure he'd heard it too, then pulled out his sidearm and made his way towards the Quonset. He moved quickly but carefully, trying to minimize his profile. As he approached the collection of squad cars parked outside the metal hut, a man appeared from the entrance of the Quonset with an assault rifle in hand. The man paused only long enough to take a breath before he took aim at Vigor and started firing.

Vigor heard one bullet zip past his head while others caromed off the cruiser he was hiding behind, but he wasn't afraid. In that moment, all the combat skills he'd learned throughout his career, especially as a fully trained tactical officer, took over. With secure cover behind one of the squad cars, Vigor smoothly pulled his automatic pistol up with both hands, took aim and started to squeeze the trigger.

"It was just a matter of self-preservation, to stop him from killing me and my partner and then, in all likelihood, hunkering down and waiting for other members," Vigor said later.

He couldn't tell if any of his rounds had hit the man who had come out of the Quonset hut firing, but Vigor's return fire, accurate or not, was enough to drive the gunman back. Almost as quickly as he had appeared, the man retreated into the Quonset.

Vigor shouted to his partner to make sure he was okay. His partner was already on the move, driving their vehicle farther onto the property to provide cover for Vigor, who raised his radio to his lips and called for backup, reporting what had just happened. Once he was assured that help was on the way, Vigor used his radio to call to the members in hut, the same four men who had greeted him only a few moments earlier. He tried again and again and again.

But all he heard was static

~

Vigor and his partner kept trying their radios, calling for any kind of response from the four officers who had gone inside. But there was no answer.

By now the entire area was surrounded by as many police officers as the local detachments could muster, toting rifles and shotguns, effectively sealing off the area. It was still early—only an hour had passed since Vigor had come under fire, but there was still no response from the Quonset, either from the officers inside or from the man who had come out shooting.

The officers couldn't storm the building as there were too many unknowns. Although the property was Roszko's and there was a chance that he was the shooter, there was also the possibility that he was not acting alone. Assuming the worst—that Johnston, Myrol, Schiemann and Gordon were all injured or dead—meant something terrible had to have happened inside, something that forced four highly trained RCMP officers to be overcome or subdued.

The property itself didn't lend itself to an immediate assault either. There was a lot of open space between where the police were and the opening of the Quonset. A vast field of fire existed for the shooter or shooters to use in any counterattack, meaning more officers would be putting their lives in danger to get to the hut. According to Vigor's account later, the weapon the gunman had was powerful and rapid-firing, either a semi-automatic that fired a round with each squeeze of the trigger and no need to cock it, or a fully automatic weapon, which could fire multiple rounds with a single pull on the trigger. The police on scene were equipped with their sidearms, shotguns and long guns, but they had nothing that could match that kind of firepower. Their bulletproof vests could stop a knife or a bullet from a handgun, but they were no match for a high-powered rifle, especially at close range.

By 10:19 AM, it was clear the Mayerthorpe detachment, in concert with the Whitecourt detachments and other surrounding police stations, did not have the training or firepower to assault the Quonset. At that point, the officers on scene finally put in a call to K Division, requesting the response of the Emergency Response Team (ERT). More commonly known in the public lexicon as a SWAT team, the members of the ERT—like Vigor himself—were highly trained in standoff situations, close combat and the use of automatic and heavy weapons. If anyone was going to figure out how to handle the situation as it was unfolding, the ERT was the best unit for it.

The officers on scene didn't stop there—they were determined to cover all their bases. A dog handler was called in to track anyone who tried to leave the area, or to conduct a high-risk takedown that might endanger the lives of the officers on scene. An explosive unit, complete with a bomb robot, was called in case there were any explosives or volatile materials that needed to be dealt with professionally. The team requested a helicopter on scene to help monitor the area from the sky and track anyone or any vehicle that tried to approach or leave the scene. The airspace immediately over the property was ordered closed to all civilian air traffic for safety reasons. Roadblocks were set up at all points of access to the property, allowing only police vehicles through. For all intents and purposes, the entire area outside James Roszko's farm was shutdown from the ground up and surrounded.

The ERT arrived on scene as quickly it could, comprised of officers who performed normal policing duties but were always on call any time the response of an ERT was warranted. As they arrived, they assembled their team and their gear—ERT members donned their black full-body armour and prepared their submachine guns for use, as well as other weapons, such as shotguns, flash-bang grenades and various assault devices.

Their assessment of the situation, however, was just as dire as that of the officers who had originally arrived on scene. The area around the Quonset was a prime kill zone, a wide-open field of fire that gave the tactical advantage to the shooter or shooters inside. Any assault, no matter how fast, involved covering a lot of ground and exposed the ERT members to gunfire, made worse still by the reports of the possible calibre of weapon that had been used earlier.

In order to approach the Quonset to successfully conduct an assault, the team was going to need some sort of cover. The RCMP cruisers on scene, though sturdy, wouldn't provide enough cover for all the ERT members, and the ERT itself, unlike many of its counterparts in the United States, did not own or have access to an armoured personnel carrier (APC). If they had an APC, the team could use it to approach the Quonset. Only someone armed with an anti-tank weapon would be able to take out such a heavily armoured vehicle.

The police, however, knew of a group of individuals several thousand members strong who did have an APC—the Canadian Forces, more specifically the army. The closest base, unfortunately, was at Canadian Forces Base (CFB) Edmonton, just northeast of the provincial capital. Any APC would require more than two hours travelling time to reach the area, but the officers on scene didn't have any choice. They needed protection if they were going to assault the hut, and the added firepower of a military vehicle's own armaments, plus the soldiers who deployed with them, would also be beneficial if a firefight occurred. Shortly after noon, the RCMP on scene put in a call to CFB Edmonton, also referred to as Edmonton Garrison.

Within minutes, two APCs, a field ambulance and 20 armed soldiers were dispatched to the scene in Mayerthorpe.

Meanwhile, there was still no response from inside the hut, and the officers inside were still not answering calls to their radios. There was no detectable movement near the opening of the Quonset hut, nor any audible sounds emanating from inside. While the team on site couldn't see far into the hut, they did see one disturbing sight—the body of one of their own officers was sprawled in the entryway of the Quonset. Ever since the call had gone out requesting backup, they'd been able to see that officer, but they couldn't identify him. And during that entire time, the officer hadn't moved.

The key concern that held up any assault on the Quonset was the possibility that there was more than one shooter, and they didn't know where that individual might be. Other officers were talking to people who knew James Roszko to try to gather as much insight into the man's frame of mind as possible. They knew Roszko was an expert marksman, and they knew he likely had a high-powered, rapid-fire weapon on his person, if he was the shooter inside. But there was little else the officers knew.

But members of the ERT were able to devise another way of extracting more intelligence from the scene. The bomb squad who arrived at the property had a remotely controlled robot that was usually deployed to inspect packages of a potentially dangerous origin, thereby diminishing the risk for bomb squad officers to inspect it personally. The robot was equipped with a camera that could also be remotely operated and provide a live feed to the officers on the outskirts of the property. The team quickly decided to send the robot in to see what it could find.

At 2:00 PM, the robot began wheeling its way across the property towards the Quonset hut, operated by its handlers at the edge of the property. Everyone gathered around the monitor to watch as the robot crossed the threshold of the Quonset's entrance, waiting anxiously to see what was going on inside.

The robot's camera panned the room as much as it would allow. The camera showed that aside from the hut being filled with miscellaneous items, the lighting conditions inside weren't ideal. The lighting was good enough, however, for the officers to see exactly what they didn't want to. As the robot panned the room, the Mounties watching the remote feed counted three of the four police officers, all crumpled to the floor, as well as the still form of a man many believed was James Roszko.

Once the situation inside the Quonset became clear, the ERT members reacted quickly. Within 15 minutes they had geared up and were running towards the hut according to a pre-planned strategy. With submachine guns at the ready, the officers breached the hut, flashlights slung under their gun barrels searching the shadows for the possible existence of another shooter. Other members of the team grabbed Gordon, Myrol, Schiemann and Johnston from where they lay and pulled or carried them as quickly as they could outside of the Quonset, then dropped down beside them to assess their condition.

The sight was heartbreaking. It didn't take a doctor or even a paramedic to know that all four officers were dead and likely had been for several hours.

So too was the man they believed was James Roszko.

The two APCs and one field ambulance on their way to the property were informed that their presence was no longer required, and they returned to base. This was a crime scene now, and it needed to be processed properly. An aerial photo taken of the scene in front of the Quonset showed four unmistakable human forms covered by sheets, now lifeless.

The news, when it came, overwhelmed the hardiest of police officers. At the command post in Mayerthorpe, a woman started screaming and collapsed into the arms of another officer. Every RCMP officer on scene felt their eyes brim with tears as they tried to stomach the gut-wrenching reality—four of their brothers-in-arms had just been killed on duty.

At that moment, an entire nation began to mourn.

The press, especially out of Edmonton, were making their way towards Mayerthorpe when they first received word of the magnitude of the situation in the small town. No sooner did the RCMP confirm the deaths of all four officers and a man than the news hit wire services, TV and radio stations first in Alberta, then across the country.

Canadians, especially residents of Mayerthorpe and those who knew the officers best, reacted in shock.

"It is with profound sadness that I confirm that four members of the Royal Canadian Mounted Police were killed today in service to our country. It is an unprecedented and unspeakable loss," said RCMP Commissioner Giuliano Zaccardelli during a statement.

"Canadians are shocked by this brutality and join me in condemning the violent acts that brought about these deaths," said Prime Minister Paul Martin.

While the RCMP did their best to control the flow of information from the scene, word was starting to get out, especially in Whitecourt and Mayerthorpe, on just who had died. Early on, the media reported that one of the dead was Constable Brock Myrol, who had been on the force for less than three weeks. The RCMP, however, did not confirm the information at first.

"We must respect the process of the medical examiner," said Corporal Wayne Oakes, a public relations officer for K Division. The medical examiner would be conducting autopsies on all four victims plus the man believed to be James Roszko.

Back in Mayerthorpe, many were angry by what had happened, but few were surprised.

"I'm sick. I don't know what to tell you. It shocks that this could even happen," said Mayerthorpe Mayor Albert Schalm.

"The cops have known him for a long time. The justice system doesn't have the balls to do what needed to be done," said Pat Burns, a local carpenter whose son had once received a jacket from Roszko. Burns had sent it back with a note telling Roszko to stay away from his son.

Members of Roszko's immediate family were also chiming in with their thoughts on what had happened. Even James' father, who hadn't seen his son in nine years, referred to him as a "wicked devil."

"I feel awful. It's most terrible what happened. I'm very much against the way James lived and went about and the way he was in jail....I feel he's not my son," said Bill Roszko.

James' brother George, who lived in Whitecourt, hadn't seen James in 15 years.

"Man alive, this is just horrible...I just feel terrible for the police," George said.

Many were quick to point out to the press that the Quonset had been the site of a marijuana grow-operation, and everyone, from the attorney general for British Columbia to RCMP Commissioner Zaccardelli himself, weighed in on the issue.

"They are high risk issues and major organized crime in many cases is involved. This is a plague on our society now,"

Zaccardelli said. He later apologized for his remarks, claiming
he was reacting based on what little information he had at the
time.

With every day came a new revelation. First, the RCMP
released a rough time line of the events leading up to the shooting, then the names of the officers and the suspect involved.
Then, on Saturday, March 5, Superintendent Marty Cheliak
held a press conference, where he revealed that all four officers
had been killed by James Roszko, that Roszko had been struck
by return fire, and that Roszko ultimately "took his own life" by
shooting himself in the chest. In the meantime, the force tried
to defend its actions that day.

"We had every reason to believe [Roszko] was not there,"
Corporal Oakes said.

Churches in Mayerthorpe on Sunday, March 6, were
packed as religious leaders addressed the actions of the previous
week. Many implored their worshippers to also pray for the soul
of the gunman, while also calling for the tougher treatment of
convicted criminals and more support for rural RCMP
detachments.

"There is anger in this community," said Arnie Laholz,
pastor for the local Pentecostal church.

Some members of the Roszko family even attended services in Whitecourt, lighting a candle at the Baptist church in
memory of the four officers. The murders were very personal,

especially for James' brother John, whose son Michael was a constable with the Edmonton Police Service.

Anger was starting to bubble over in Mayerthorpe, especially as the press, now occupying almost every available hotel room, scattered throughout the community, looking for fresh angles and stories. At one point, a reporter who tried to question an officer leaving the detachment was punched in the face. Some chastised the press for their presence, while others were happy to have them, stating that if they weren't there, no one would know anything about what was going on.

The deaths of Myrol, Schiemann and Johnston constituted the bulk of the Mayerthorpe detachment's manpower, while Gordon's death shocked his detachment in Whitecourt. Those left behind were reeling, grieving for their lost comrades. Other RCMP detachments from across Alberta dispatched officers to Mayerthorpe to take over the policing duties. Mounties with specialized training in organizing roadblocks and in crowd control were also sent to the area as a precaution. Already the RCMP had been forced to intercept James' youngest brother Doug who, when he heard of Roszko's demise, angrily declared that he was going to do something about it and took off in his truck for James' property. An alert brother of Doug's contacted the RCMP, who stopped Doug before he could reach his destination.

Not every member of the Roszko family was quick to condemn James. His mother Stephanie and sister Josephine Ruel had been close to Roszko.

"My biggest regret is that I didn't tell him I loved him," Josephine told the press, referring to a long phone conversation she'd had with James the night before the tragedy began to unfold.

The detachments at Mayerthorpe and Whitecourt became small shrines to the officers as local residents and other Albertans dropped off flowers, wreaths, teddy bears and cards to commemorate the four officers. Books of condolence were set up at every RCMP detachment, including the rotunda of the Provincial Legislature in Edmonton, and the public was encouraged to sign. Plans were already in the works for a large memorial service in Edmonton, at the University of Alberta's indoor track facility, otherwise known as the "Butterdome," for Thursday, March 10. Protocol officers scrambled to get everything in place, as thousands of police officers from across North America were expected to attend, along with the prime minister, governor general, premier of Alberta and other dignitaries.

~

Meanwhile, back at Roszko's property, the investigation continued.

Forensics officers combed as much of the property as possible, looking for cigarette butts, footprints or any other kind of telltale evidence that could explain the one burning question that was foremost in the minds of the investigating officers: if James Roszko had been seen leaving the property, how did he get back inside the hut without anyone knowing?

The truck the bailiffs had originally come searching for, the one in which Roszko was seen leaving the property, was also found, in a hamlet 20 kilometres away in his aunt's garage. Its discovery added even more of an element of intrigue to the question of how Roszko got back onto the property—if his truck was ditched so far away from the crime scene, how had he been able to get back to his own property in time to sneak into the Quonset and shoot the four officers? The police appealed to the public for any information they might have about the intervening hours between Roszko's departure and the shootings. Specifically, they wanted to try to establish whether Roszko had hiked the 20 kilometres back to the farm himself or if he had hitched a ride with either a knowing, unwitting or uncooperative accomplice.

By Tuesday, March 9, the press began to leave Mayerthorpe. The story wasn't finished though, it had just moved. Constable Peter Schiemann was going to be the first officer to be buried.

Don Schiemann had baptized his son and had confirmed him. And now he was going to bury him.

Approximately 2400 officers turned up for Peter Schiemann's funeral in Stony Plain, Alberta, on Tuesday, March 8, marching to the church in uniform to the sound of the Edmonton Pipes and Drums band. Overflow crowds watched the service from one of the high school's two gymnasiums.

Two days later, the entire country seemed to grind to a halt as the memorial at the University of Alberta began. In total, 10,000 police officers, emergency workers and border guards, from British Colombia to New Jersey, attended. Edmontonians opened their homes to the officers, offering to billet those from out of town. Hotels were already starting to fill up because of the sheer number of police officers attending.

Citizens started lining up at 8:00 that morning, hoping to get a seat for the service. Overflows were diverted into the Clare Drake Arena, which had a television screen set up inside. Outside the Butterdome, a gigantic Canadian flag hung at half-mast from a construction crane. Beneath it, four black ribbons attached to the crane snapped in the breeze.

The procession began at Emily Murphy Park as the assembled officers marched one kilometre to the indoor stadium as hundreds of spectators lining the route watched. The CBC broadcast the ceremony live—four candles burned on stage as four officers on horseback brought in the Guidon, the RCMP's regimental flag, which was laid across a traditional bass drum. Four friends marched in the four Stetsons belonging to Anthony Gordon, Peter Schiemann, Leo Johnston and Brock Myrol, which were placed on horse blankets that rested in front of a portrait of each of the four officers.

In turn, all four officers were eulogized by the people who knew them best. Johnston's twin brother Lee called him "my brother, my best friend and the most important person in my life." Constable Barrie Baskerville remembered Gordon as a "friendly, gentle giant of a man, both physically and in the way he cared for those he encountered as a policeman doing his job."

Family friend Pastor Art Hundeby described Myrol as "driven as a child, driven as a teen and in overdrive as an adult."

Don Schiemann found it hard to sum up his son in so few words.

"If you want to know my son, you'll need to come to our home and we'll put on a large pot of coffee and talk for hours," Don said.

Various politicians and bureaucrats had their turn before the memorial came to a close. Each individual officer also had private services limited to family and friends, each filled with gut-wrenching moments. At Myrol's service in Red Deer, his fiancée bent over and kissed the casket before it was carted away.

"I would gladly have given my life for Brock for so many reasons," said friend Shane McCambridge.

On Friday, March 11, Leo Johnston was laid to rest in Lac La Biche. Approximately 1500 people attended the service before his burial in the northern Alberta town.

"He was full of adventure and ambition," said Richard Cadieu, Johnston's former high school teacher.

The last funeral drew the least notice. Not even 12 people showed up at a Mayerthorpe funeral home to say goodbye to James Roszko; a service organized by his sister Josephine Ruel.

"The focus is on what led up to the tragedy," she said. "I don't regret saying I loved my brother."

Most of the Roszko family chose not to attend.

"This little weirdo came along and screwed everything up. You've got to wonder what the hell happened to him," his brother George said.

On Tuesday, March 15, the town of Mayerthorpe finally got its chance to grieve at a public service. Approximately 1500 people attended the service at a local school, which was marked by music and PowerPoint presentations by students. Even John Roszko, one of James' brothers, attended.

The services and memorials were over, but the investigation continued.

∾

On March 16, the press was able to answer some questions about how Roszko got back to his Quonset undetected. The *National Post*, using an anonymous source, reported that Roszko had used a white sheet to camouflage himself in the snow as he approached the property. The source also indicated Roszko wore heavy socks over his boots, which helped mask the sound of his own footsteps from the officers who were guarding the property. Roszko had been shot four times—two of the bullets had entered each side of his groin, one had hit a revolver he'd tucked into his front waistband, and the fourth had struck the stock of his Heckler & Koch assault rifle. The rifle was a semi-automatic with a 20-round magazine, larger than legally allowed in Canada.

The families of the fallen officers, specifically the Schiemann and Myrol families, became vocal opponents of liberalized drug laws. Former Prime Minister Jean Chrétien had tabled legislation in the House of Commons that would decriminalize small amounts of marijuana while increasing prison time for people found growing the drug. The bill quietly disappeared from Parliament and was never enacted. The families asked Canadians to leave their porch lights burning, starting from October 3, and to do so on the third day of every month until March 3.

On December 7, the CBC investigative news program *The Fifth Estate* broadcast a documentary dedicated to the Mayerthorpe shootings, alleging the sequence of events released by the RCMP was false. Entitled *A Hail of Bullets*, the documentary argued that the officers did not know how dangerous Roszko was, that Roszko had snuck into the hut while the officers were drugging the dogs, even though there was no evidence to corroborate the statement. It also alleged that Myrol had been the only officer shot inside the Quonset; that Gordon and Schiemann had been shot outside and that Johnston had been able to fire one round before he died, which struck the gun in Roszko's waistband. The CBC stated they came to these conclusions based on "available information," including aerial photos of the crime scene that showed the bodies outside the hut.

The program went even further, arguing that the police search of the Quonset had been illegal, that the RCMP had known of the grow-op for some time and were looking for an excuse to get on the property. It also suggested Roszko had once killed a witness in a case against him. The man had actually fallen down a staircase.

The RCMP did not assist with the documentary, and its conclusions were widely panned.

Over the next two years, the amount of information made available to the public seemed to dry up, leading many to wonder if there was any kind of ongoing investigation at all. A Crown review of Roszko's criminal record in October 2005 revealed that Roszko had been flagged as a potential dangerous offender, but no more serious convictions ever came.

"It's aggravating to read this and knew he got away with this stuff. The more I read, the more upset I get," said Doreen Duffy, Gordon's mother, after she had reviewed the report.

The province had ordered a fatality inquiry, but it had to wait until the investigation itself was complete. The fact that there was an ongoing investigation was only revealed in October 2006 when the media successfully petitioned a Court of Queen's Bench judge to unseal a series of warrants that had been originally sealed by a lower court without notifying the media first. The information in the warrants showed that the RCMP was working under the assumption that Roszko had help. Cell phone records for the time period James was on the run showed he called his aunt between 2:30 and 3:00 AM on March 3, looking for his mother. His aunt said the call display on her phone showed the call came from an "S. Hennessey," later identified as Shawn Hennessey of Barrhead, Alberta. Roszko's aunt alleged Hennessey was an acquaintance of James.

The warrants also stated that Hennessey received several calls on March 2 from Roszko, who was looking for somewhere to hide his truck. Hennessey refused his request, and when Roszko showed up at his home anyway, Hennessey's wife allegedly turned him away.

"Hennessey is a person on which Roszko would turn for assistance," the warrant stated.

The media contacted Shawn Hennessey, who refused to comment.

The warrants revealed that Roszko had called his aunt again later that morning, stating he had made a will and that everyone should pray for him. Earlier that evening, Roszko's mom Stephanie had called her sister and asked if Roszko could stash the truck at her place, to which she agreed.

In total, the police seized 199 items from Roszko's farm, including 12 guns, a crossbow, police scanners, pepper spray and handcuffs. They found a handwritten list of officers serving with the Mayerthorpe, Evansburg and Whitecourt detachments, along with the call signs of the vehicles usually assigned to each member and the cell phone associated with the vehicle. They also discovered that one of the guns recovered had been stolen from the father of a "drug associate." The officers' families expressed their dismay that the warrants were unsealed, believing the information might tip off whatever accomplices there might be.

In January 2007, a workplace safety report of the incident was finally completed. It stated that Roszko alone was responsible for the deaths of all four officers. It also called for heavier ceramic body armour for the force, as well as night vision goggles and better radios.

More importantly, the report discredited many of the findings in the CBC documentary. The officers all knew that Roszko was dangerous. The report also revealed that Roszko had been hiding behind a 1000-gallon plastic container inside the Quonset when the officers walked in, and that Johnston had been the only officer to return fire, striking Roszko once.

The unsealing of the warrants was proof that an investigation into the shootings was ongoing—eight officers were working on the case. Finally, on Sunday, June 8, 2007, the RCMP announced the arrests of Shawn Hennessey and Dennis Cheeseman of Barrhead. The pair, who were related through marriage, were caught in an undercover investigation and charged with four counts of first-degree murder.

"The fact that it took 28 months to get to this point speaks to the fact that every case is unique," said Deputy Commissioner Bill Sweeney.

The town was shocked by the arrests. Hennessey worked at the Kal-Tire in Barrhead, a business that Roszko frequented. According to friends and family, Shawn had once been a bit of a drinker and a fighter but had since married and had two daughters.

"There's no story with Shawn. It's been almost a year now and if the police had anything on him, they would have charged him," said his boss Steve Hunter.

The arrest warrants also alleged that Hennessey had sold drugs for Roszko.

"He didn't do nothing as far as I'm concerned," Hunter added.

Cheeseman had been a team leader at Sepallo, a local company that made fruit and vegetable powders. He lived with Hennessey and was described as a "shy, naive man young man with a huge heart."

The pair's first court appearance was on July 13, 2007, in Mayerthorpe, but their lawyers appeared for them. The packed courtroom watched as a man clutching a Bible, describing himself as an "ambassador of the kingdom of heaven," stood and announced, "I have some new evidence that should be on the record." When the judge told him he couldn't interrupt, the man asked if the court "is trying to hide something."

The sense in Barrhead was one of disbelief that either man had anything to do with the Mayerthorpe shootings. The town held bake sales and fundraisers to raise money for their defence.

"It's just a big political thing because they have got lots of pressure to come down on somebody," said Chris Gordon, who watched the first appearance from the gallery.

It later came to light that Hennessey and Cheeseman may have been arrested during an undercover operation known as the "Mr. Big Sting," a tactic outlawed in the United States and Great Britain. Both men were allegedly approached by undercover police officers claiming to belong to an illegal organization. They allegedly plied both men with booze, money, drugs and prostitutes in exchange for doing small favours for them. Finally, on July 6, 2007, Hennessey and Cheeseman were scheduled to meet "Mr. Big," the head of the organization, to whom they had to confess all their crimes in order to prove their trustworthiness.

∼

The Mr. Big operation wasn't the only strange matter developing. In Lac La Biche, a new battleground had formed over the gravesite of Leo Johnston. Although Johnston had been buried in Lac La Biche, his widow, Kelly, had learned of the RCMP cemetery in Regina and decided that's where Leo should be buried. As legislation gives spouses precedence in making such decisions, an exhumation order was granted. Leo's family was horrified and fought the exhumation as far as they could, claiming Leo had told his brother Lee he wanted to be buried in Lac La Biche.

"This is what I believe in my heart are my husband's true wishes," Kelly said.

When Leo's parents' appeal of the order was thrown out in court, friends and family blockaded the gravesite in October 2007 until an RCMP officer showed up and informed the group the exhumation would not be taking place. The matter was put before the Alberta Court of Appeal in November 2007, which ruled that Johnston's remains could be moved to Regina. Leo's parents vowed to file an appeal with the Supreme Court of Canada.

~

On March 1, 2008, Constable Steve Vigor was awarded the Medal of Bravery by the Governor General for his role in helping stop James Roszko.

"I would much rather have the four officers here," Vigor said.

~

Within a month of one another, both Shawn Hennessey and Dennis Cheeseman were granted bail, under hefty financial sureties and strict conditions, one of which was that they not associate with each other. A preliminary hearing began, but the proceedings were blacked out by a publication ban. At the end of the hearing, which came on June 6, 2008, Hennessey and Cheeseman were ordered to stand trial. Both men started to cry when the decision was handed down.

The pair is scheduled to enter pleas in September 2008. The trial has been tentatively scheduled to run from April 5 to June 19, 2009.

On July 5, 2008, under sunny skies and with thousands present, a memorial to the fallen four officers was finally unveiled in Mayerthorpe. Built in part with government grant money and funds raised through various donations, the Fallen Four Memorial features statues of all four officers and a seven-metre-tall memorial dedicated to all police officers, firefighters and soldiers across Canada. The total cost of construction added up to $1.8 million.

While some, like Jason Gordon, Anthony Gordon's brother, criticized the monument as "a black mark" on the town, many others hailed it as a proper dedication to the four officers. Even Prime Minister Stephen Harper attended the opening, remarking on the significance of the new monument.

"The constables did not die in vain."

Notes on Sources

Dennis Strongquill

McIntyre, Mike. "Mountie's Killer Set for Release Despite Concerns." *Winnipeg Free Press,* February 13, 2008.

———*Nowhere to Run: The Killing of Constable Dennis Strongquill.* Winnipeg: Great Plains Publications, 2003.

Perreaux, Les. "Slain Mountie 'Was a Lover, Not a Fighter.'" *National Post*, December 28, 2001.

Scott, Neil, and Michelle Lang. "RCMP Shooting Suspects Face Murder Charges." *The StarPhoenix*, December 24, 2001.

Staples, David. "Accused Killer Attacks Lawyer: Jury Missed Violent Outburst." *Edmonton Journal*, June 13, 2003.

———"Cop Killer's Lover Gets 10 Years." *Edmonton Journal*, July 2, 2003.

———"Fearless, Painless, Senseless: The Sand Brothers." *Edmonton Journal*, March 31, 2002.

———"No Time to Call in Negotiators: Mountie." *CanWest News Service*, April 24, 2003.

———"Sand, Bell Guilty. Mountie Gunned Down in 'Cowardly Slaughter,' Judge." *Edmonton Journal*, June 14, 2003.

James Galloway

Brooymans, Hanneke. "Accident Left Gunman 'Haunted by Voices.'" *Edmonton Journal*, March 1, 2004.

Cormier, Ryan. "Shooter's Family, Health Groups Hail Findings: Mountie Rammed Pickup to Keep Suspect from Escaping." *Edmonton Journal*, November 22, 2006.

——"Standoff Strategy Blamed in Mountie Death." *Edmonton Journal*, November 15, 2005.

D'Aliesio, Renata, and Jessica Leeder. "Slain Mountie Laid to Rest." *Edmonton Journal*, March 6, 2004.

Honourable Judge Peter Ayotte. "Report to the Minister of Justice and Attorney General, Public Fatality Inquiry." November 3, 2006.

Staples, David. "Tracking an RCMP Legend." *Edmonton Journal*, March 6, 2005.

Robin Cameron and Marc Bourdages

Adam, Betty Ann. "Dagenais to Stand Trial for Murder." *The Leader-Post*, August 22, 2007.

Bernhardt, Darren. "Praying for a Miracle: Injured Mountie's Family Waiting by Her Bedside; Manhunt for Dagenais Continues near Spiritwood." *The StarPhoenix*, July 11, 2006.

Bernhardt, Darren, and Sarah MacDonald. "2 Mounties Shot in Saskatchewan: Seriously Injured." *The StarPhoenix*, July 9, 2006.

Saccone, Julie. "Suspect Known in Hometown as Police Hater." *The StarPhoenix*, July 10, 2006.

Saccone, Julie, and Darren Bernhardy. "RCMP Believes Shooting Suspect Still in Dragnet Zone." *The StarPhoenix*, July 13, 2006.

Warick, Jason, and Julie Saccone. "Dagenais Confused in Court." *The Leader-Post*, July 20, 2006.

——"Letter Blames Police for Shooting." *The StarPhoenix*, July 19, 2006.

Wood, Jason, and Julie Saccone. "Suspect in Mountie Deaths Turns Himself in." *The StarPhoenix*, July 19, 2006.

Daniel Tessier

Bruemmer, Rene, Alan Hustak, and Anne Sutherland. "Family Mourns Future Without Father." *Montréal Gazette*, March 10, 2007.

Cherry, Paul. "Crown Won't Appeal Parasiris's Acquittal." *Montréal Gazette*, July 12, 2008.

——"Key Issue in Murder Trial: Was Cop Easily Identified?" *Montréal Gazette*, May 23, 2008.

——"Officers Testify in Raid Gone Wrong." *Montréal Gazette*, May 27, 2008.

——"Quebec Man Not Guilty in Policeman's Death." *Montréal Gazette*, June 14, 2008.

Lalonde, Michelle. "Man Faces First-Degree Murder Charge in Québec Policeman's Death." *Montréal Gazette*, March 4, 2007.

Montgomery, Sue. "He Feared for His Family." *Montréal Gazette*, March 6, 2007.

Wilton, Katherine. "Laval Cops Heart-Broken by Killing." *Montréal Gazette*, March 8, 2007.

Christopher Worden

Cormier, Ryan. "Man Found with Alleged Cop Killer." *Edmonton Journal*, October 14, 2007.

Cormier, Ryan, et al. "7-day Hunt Ends at City Townhouse." *Edmonton Journal*, October 13, 2007.

Edmonton Journal, "Accused Mountie-killer Faces More Charges." February 13, 2008.

Kleiss, Karen. "Alleged Mountie Shot Four Times in Forest Chase." *Edmonton Journal*, October 27, 2007.

Zabjek, Alexandra. "Mountie Killer's Trail Leads Out of Town." *Edmonton Journal*, October 8, 2007.

——"RCMP Name Suspect in Mountie's Shooting." *Edmonton Journal*, October 8, 2007.

Brock Myrol, Anthony Gordon, Peter Schiemann and Leo Johnston

Collins, Michelle. "Two Charged in Alberta RCMP Slayings." *Edmonton Journal*, July 9, 2007.

Cormier, Ryan. "Mountie Killer Not Dangerous Enough: Report." *Edmonton Journal*, October 6, 2005.

——"Police Mum on Accomplice." *Edmonton Journal*, November 1, 2005.

D'Aliesio, Renata, and Andrew McLean. "Bailiff Tells of Lead-up to Ambush." *Edmonton Journal*, March 6, 2005.

D'Aliesio, Renata, and David Staples. "Portrait of a Predator." *Edmonton Journal*, March 20, 2005.

D'Aliesio, Renata, et al. "A 'Wicked Devil,' a 'Nut Case.'" *Edmonton Journal*, March 4, 2005.

Edmonton Journal, "Officer's Widow Wins Fight Over Body." May 17, 2008.

Farrell, Jim. "Murdered Officer on Job Only 17 Days." *Edmonton Journal*, March 4, 2005.

Gelinas, Ben. "Trial Set in Mayerthorpe Slayings." *Edmonton Journal*, June 7, 2008.

Humphreys, Adrian. "Roszko Used White Sheet to Stalk Mounties." *National Post,* March 16, 2005.

Johnsrude, Larry. "He Joined Force after Recovering from Accident." *Edmonton Journal*, March 5, 2005.

Loyie, Florence, and Mike Sadava. "Four Cops Killed: Alta. Officers Shot During Grow-op Raid." *Edmonton Journal*, March 4, 2005.

O'Donnell, Sarah, and Ryan Cormier. "Police Knew Killer was a Risk, Warrant Shows." *Edmonton Journal*, March 5, 2005.

Sinnema, Jodie. "Concern for Other was Reinforced by Faith." *Edmonton Journal*, March 5, 2005.

——"Constable's Life revolved around RCMP." *Edmonton Journal*, March 5, 2005.

Sinnema, Jodie, et al. "Constables Returned Fire—Gunman Killed Himself." *Edmonton Journal*, March 6, 2006.

Peter Boer

In his position as assistant editor and as a reporter for the *St. Albert Gazette*, Peter Boer has covered everything from city council meetings to crime. His on-the-job experience, much of which has been spent in courtrooms throughout the Capital region in Edmonton, as well as his background in psychology, has led him to a fascination with the bigger picture of crime in Canada. He has examined both its roots and the effects of crime on people on a local and national scale. Boer has penned seven other non-fiction titles, and his successful storytelling style draws the reader into the lives of the people he portrays.